AI and the Challenge to Literary Studies

Tim Lanzendörfer

AI and the Challenge to Literary Studies

palgrave
macmillan

Tim Lanzendörfer
Goethe University
Frankfurt am Main, Germany

ISBN 978-3-032-25525-9 ISBN 978-3-032-25526-6 (eBook)
https://doi.org/10.1007/978-3-032-25526-6

This Palgrave Macmillan imprint is published by the registered company Springer Nature Switzerland AG.
The registered company address is: Gewerbestrasse 11, 6330 Cham, Switzerland

To Anselma, Anton, and Marlene

Preface

What would it mean for AI to solve literary studies? How you react to this question may be the first indication for how you will read this book, in very much the same way that the advent of large-language model, generative AI exposes the fault lines of the discipline of literary studies in the contemporary. You may bristle at the notion that there is anything to "solve" in literary studies in the first place—insist that both literature and the work of literary studies, already implicitly interwoven in form, aren't something that can be done by a machine, or that texts cannot be said to have "solutions" the way that, say, physics questions have. So while you may grant that, as the cheerleaders of AI have it, physics, or protein folding, or mathematics might be solved by AI, literature and literary studies are not likely to be solved—to be done away with—by AI's advent. Or, if you hold with the possibility that much of literary studies work might in fact be doable by AI, that might still not mean anything—that it just will not matter in practice. Or, perhaps, you might be intrigued by the very question: what might thinking about the question yield, as far as insights into literary studies are concerned? (What would it mean to ask the question: What would it mean for AI to solve literary studies?) I explore what the advent of large-language model, generative artificial intelligence confronts the field of literary studies with. I argue that we cannot avoid the question because we share with LLM, generative AI our nature as producers of texts from other texts. I develop my major claim that we must stop thinking in terms of our outputs in the form of an essay, and progress from a discussion of AI (and other) literature to gestures toward our disciplinary future. I ask you to follow along as I raise concerns about our understanding of literature, of the nature of literary studies, and the ways in which AI may help or hinder us, or indeed make literary studies work pointless—or, perhaps, merely highlight how pointless it has always been.

Frankfurt am Main, Germany
Tim Lanzendörfer

Acknowledgments

I want to thank Philipp Löffler and Laura Bieger for the invitation to the conference "What was the Contemporary," held in September 2024 at the University of Heidelberg, Germany, at which I was able to present the initial thoughts on genAI from which this book has sprung. Thanks, especially, to the participants at that conference for their valuable feedback, comments, arguments, and encouragement.

Kieran Chart helpfully discussed elements of real-world genAI use cases and latest developments as this book took final shape.

Nir Evron provided copious commentary on the book, strong encouragement of its main thesis, and helpful additional suggestions.

Two early commentators on the conference paper proved especially valuable interlocutors, both for their initial push toward publication and later efforts at making better what I wrote. Adam Kelly offered trenchant critique on the whole and provided helpful corrections and emendations, excellent ideas for further sources and useful commentary—not all of which I took on board, admittedly. Lee Konstantinou read the whole manuscript and suggested helpful emendations, changes, additional reading, and suggestions for structural alternatives that I also did not completely adopt, but which helped stimulate my thoughts. As the progenitors of the entire idea to put these thoughts into print, I am much in their debt.

Torsten Schmidt was one of the earliest readers of the manuscript and offered trenchant insights into its shortcomings as well as supportive words where things worked.

To the anonymous reviewers at Palgrave, my thanks for their careful and occasionally challenging reads.

Thanks to the staff and faculty at the American Studies department, Institute of English and American Studies, Goethe University, Frankfurt, a temporary academic home that, nonetheless, feels like a home. Thanks for taking me in!

Work on this book was made possible by the extreme liberality of the German Research Foundation's Heisenberg program, under whose funding title *Reading in the Age of Trump: The Practices, Possibilities, and Futures of Literary Studies Now* (LA 4020/3–1) my work was undertaken. Artificial intelligence was not a major concern for the futures of literary studies when I began work on that project, and it is the malleability of the program that permits me to do this work now—for whatever it is worth.

Finally, thanks to my family: Anselma, Anton, and Marlene. You're letting me do this thing that nobody really gets, and I'm not sure I fully get, at least a little while longer.

Competing Interests The author has no competing interests to declare that are relevant to the content of this manuscript.

Contents

About the Author

Tim Lanzendörfer is Heisenberg Researcher for Literary Theory, Literary Studies, and Literary Studies Education in the American Studies Department at Goethe University, Frankfurt, Germany. He is the author of three other monographs, including *Utopian Pasts and Futures in the Contemporary American Novel* (Edinburgh University Press, 2023), as well as several collections of essays, including *The Futures of Literary Criticism* (Palgrave Macmillan, 2025, with Mathias Nilges) and *The Medial Afterlives of H.P: Lovecraft* (Palgrave Macmillan, 2023, with Max Dreysse). His current work is on the value of public literary studies and the challenges to literary studies' futures.

CHAPTER 1

Introduction

Abstract This introduction lays out the fundamental assumptions and arguments of the present volume. Drawing inspiration from Benjamin Labatut's novel *The MANIAC*, it suggests that contemporary discussions around generative artificial intelligence in literary studies are insufficiently attuned to the ways in which genAI will potentially impact literary studies beyond the question of how it will impact the writing of literary texts—namely, in the production of literary studies texts. The introduction lays out the connections the book explores further on between different ways literary studies has recently adopted to understand literature as well as its own epistemologies. It suggests that key terms in recent revisions of literary studies, notably creativity and craft, will have to figure differently in a post-genAI world—but that, at the same time, the genAI moment allows us to profitably re-engage the question of literary studies practices.

Keywords Literary studies • Literary theory • Creativity • Literary sociology • Artificial intelligence • Literature • Craft

Imagine the following: it's October 2029, and there's news from Stockholm. There's a new winner of the Nobel Prize in Literature, and his name is Sam Altman, CEO of OpenAI, the firm that developed ChatGPT. The Committee's citation reads, quite simply, something like

T. Lanzendörfer, *AI and the Challenge to Literary Studies*,
https://doi.org/10.1007/978-3-032-25526-6_1

the following: "for generating several lifetimes' worth of literature in the span of the past few years, signally expanding what it means to write literature, and setting new standards of creativity." You may bristle. Even coming in the wake of Google/DeepMind's shared win of the Nobel Prize in Chemistry in 2024, and John J. Hopfield and Geoffrey Hinton's winning in the Physics category for machine learning and neural networks themselves, this future Nobel for ChatGPT *feels* wrong, I think—but why?

Perhaps it's possible to situate this feeling a little better. We would probably all prefer to not think about art—creativity, originality, innovation—including the writing of literature as a stochastic enterprise, and for various reasons I do not personally think that ChatGPT or any of its successors or competitors will win the Nobel Prize in literature (not even through an intermediate such as Altman). That has to do in no small part with how we imagine our creative faculties as human faculties. But there's a different way of understanding this quality. The final section of the Chilean writer Benjamin Labatut's 2023 novel *The MANIAC* describes a match of Go, the highly complex Chinese board game which, as the novel has it, "has more board configurations than there are atoms in the universe" (2023, 300). The match, a fictionalized version of a real-life encounter, sets off the best Go player on the planet, the Korean Lee Sedol, against a computer program, AlphaGo, designed by the company DeepMind (a company now controlled by Alphabet). AlphaGo is a large neural network-based, reinforced-learning AI program. On the basis of millions of recorded games of Go and millions more games it played against itself, it has now become strong enough to beat Sedol in the match. But what's interesting is perhaps less that it wins, but how it wins, and how the novel describes that win. Toward the end of the second game it plays against Sedol, it comes up with what all expert commentators understand to be a strange move. That move is "not simply a bad move, it has been reviled and derided by the great masters and the thousands of volumes on Go written during the more than three thousand years of continuous play" (2023, 316). It is only the person that has played the most games against AlphaGo, who best knows how it was played before, who sees it "for what it really was: a stroke of genius" (317).

Sedol, I've said, loses the match. But on the way there, in the novel's telling, something intriguing happens. In the fourth of five games, he makes a move so unusual that AlphaGo cannot cope, and it goes on to lose the game. That move, Labatut's novel says, had come to Sedol "out of sheer inspiration." His "thought processes had not been rational at all," producing a move which the observing computer programs give a "probability of zero point zero zero zero one." And that, it turns out, is "exactly the same probability that AlphaGo had assigned to its own groundbreaking move" in the previous game (340–341).

Why begin a book on literary studies and AI with this novelistic exploration of a Go engine's success? *The MANIAC* is a book about the dangers of technocratic-managerial approaches to science; it's also a book about creative thinking, human genius, and how to understand it, a true story, barely a novel, a remix of historical events to suggest a particular narrative about the dangers of technology. And here, on its last couple of pages, it broaches an uncomfortable possibility: that all "genius," all "inspiration," all creativity, is at heart probabilistic, merely a matter of picking an unusual option from a sea of possibilities. And whether the rare chance is picked by a human or a computer program doesn't matter in the end: the result is, in either case, a genius move. Genius moves are winning moves—but they are indistinguishably human or AI moves, because all genius is at heart stochastic genius.

This episode might feel like it's not particular urgent: after all, we've known AI was capable of beating humans at board games at least since DeepBlue beat Garry Kasparov at chess in 1997, and what's one more board game in the grand scheme of things. But, as I want to suggest, the developments highlighted by Labatut's novel are different specifically because they can be understood in terms usually reserved for human artistic practices, because there is nothing immediately absurd about Labatut's evocation of genius in AlphaGO's success. The best reason to start with *The MANIAC* here, rather than the mere recounting of the history of the encounter between Sedol and AlphaGo, is that it is already a very particular narrative of how creativity, how genius, and how making good moves in a field actually work. These narratives are very like the narratives that literary studies constructs for itself, and which I will be talking about below. And, embellished as it is (and it is not much embellished), *The MANIAC*'s retelling of the victory of AlphaGo is also still sufficiently historically accurate: there really was this match between a Korean Go master and a computer, and the computer really won, even though the majority of observers believed it impossible. The two moves really happened. And the match had some real, personal consequences: three years after his defeat, Lee Sedol retired from playing Go—for the simple reason that he knew he would never be stronger than the computer. As he noted in the *New York Times* in 2024: "Losing to A.I., in a sense, meant my entire world was collapsing" (Wakabashi and Young 2024).

This book is about what it will mean for literary studies to potentially find its own world collapsing, a world in which textual work still matters. All the same, it is not so much about the capacities, current or future, of AI textual producers as such. It is about the questions that obtrude from the possibilities of AI as textual producer—about the potential consequences of AI, rather than the actual futures (which are, not just to me, opaque). And it's not even primarily about the question of whether or not AI does, can, or will produce "literature," though that question cannot be ignored. There has been a host of arguments about what whether or not AI can be an "author," whether or not it can ever produce "literature," and, as we will see, whether or not whatever it produces can be considered "good." These questions are somewhat ancillary to the one I am after, though they are, in a different sense that I will explore, quite fundamental. What I am interested here is the question of how literary studies, as a discipline, is impacted by the developments, current, future, and merely potential, of AI. This question, I wager, has been implicit in the background of at least some of the discussions around AI's capacity to produce literature that we have seen happening in literary studies recently. But it's still, largely, implicit, or restricted to the question of what we would do, how, with AI literature. Interest in AI and literary studies cannot fully escape the pull of contemporary thinking about AI literary production, of course. Whether or not an AI can be an "author" is important for some variants of literary studies thinking, obviously (more, I would wager, than we care to admit); and so is the category of the "literary." Yet ultimately, we need to think about the discipline itself.

This book is structured accordingly. In the first section, after a brief attempt at outlining the key terms and a very short history of AI, I will in fact tackle the question of AI literature. Specifically, from the vantage of my concerns for literary studies, I will discuss what it means to say "literature" and to write literature in the age of large-language model, neural-network, generative AI (what, for simplicity's sake, I will call "genAI" from here on out). This is important groundwork for my discussion of literary studies, because, as it turns, there are both overlapping rhetorics and overlapping theories of practice at work in literary production and literary studies work. But my focus is not on debating the question of literature as such. Rather, I foreground what I understand to be an understudied aspect of the genAI revolution we may be witnessing: what it might mean for the discipline of literary studies writ large, beyond engaging with the fact that computational writing exists. I will foreground here a concern that stands implicitly behind many of the contributions to the discussion around genAI literature. That is the question of how any of the various claims raised about the limits of genAI are actually readable in the textual outputs of genAI. This is a question that, I suggest, goes beyond the taxonomical worries around what counts as literature, and who might be considered an author. It allows us to rethink, to think again, the discipline's relation to these concerns and how they impact our understanding of what the discipline is for. Departing from this point, I want to foreground a question that, perhaps surprisingly, has barely been covered in discussions of genAI: the question of what it would mean for genAI to make our work, to generate literary studies texts. In the second section, I will address the question of what genAI means for literary studies in this specific sense. That this is necessarily tied to what genAI can be imagined to do for "literature" is, again, granted. But my point is less about the "reception of these [genAI] technologies" (Perlow 2024, 550) in a general sense. My question goes further, to the very textual practices of the discipline themselves, and thus tackles issues that have not been given a lot of thought in the discipline. If there's a unique selling point to the volume, it's that.

A rhetorically radical over-claim for reader engagement in this regard might look like this: genAI promises to make literature and literary studies as we know the terms impossible. On or about November 2022, the character of writing changed so fundamentally that doing literary studies will cease to make sense. This is an over-claim, for one, in so far as it has never really made sense to do literary studies (I partially kid). For two, what I want to do here is less argue the validity of the claim as explore the consequences of its potential validity, and how it is tied to certain understandings of literature, literary studies practices and epistemologies, and an understanding of the modes and methods of the field. The post-genAI moment we inhabit is not a moment of mourning for something lost, whatever we take our situation to be in fact, but a moment of reflexive opportunity, an opportunity that Michelle Elam has already diagnosed for the world of art production in words that fit here, too: "a bracing wake-up call to a settled status quo" (2023, 289). GenAI allows us to see with greater clarity how the things we have been doing all along are hinged on sets of assumptions, beliefs, and—to stick with genAI—hallucinations that are worth interrogating and in need of interrogation. (One of these things we do, one of those hallucinations, paradoxically, is no doubt the writing of a book.) The key intervention that genAI makes is to reveal how the issues we discuss in relation to it now in fact pertain anyway, and have always pertained. Fundamentally, these issues touch on the question of why we do work in literary studies, and what that work's purpose is.

Among the things that figure here as assumptions or beliefs around which literary studies work is organized are key terms in the complex hinted at by Labatut's novel: "inspiration" and "genius," and beyond those "originality" and "creativity"—indeed, maybe just "literariness" or "quality"—including the upshot of the fact that we tend to resist (mostly, though exceptions apply) the idea that genAI will be more than a "stochastic parrot" (Bender et al. 2021). *The MANIAC* suggests that we may be mistaken in this assumption—if not in the actually, currently existing (in early 2026) models, but as a matter of principle. I will also talk about intention, meaning, truth, and knowledge, as categories of literary studies, and the way in which they are bound up in assumptions about what literary studies should do and what literature is; and I want to talk about usefulness as an overarching promise of the discipline. These issues are all interconnected between the fields of literary production and of literary studies, and they are deeply woven into discussions of genAI.

One of the angles I want to pursue in the following is the point that recent literary studies scholarship has already gone a long but ambivalent way to decenter author figures and their creative genius. These discussions are clearly important in contextualizing what I am trying to do here (see, for instance, Evron and Tortakovsky 2024), as are perhaps more philosophical discussions around genAI and "meaning" (see for instance Kirschenbaum 2023) that clearly matter to genAI's relation to literary studies. Much that is useful has been said about these issues. But they are also only part of a much larger ongoing debate, one which includes both the question of literary production and the production of scholarship. Mark McGurl's 2009 *The Program Era*, a key text in institutional literary studies, highlights throughout the way in which the writing of literature, and in particular the "creative writing" taught in MFA programs, must reframe our thinking about individual authorial agency. The "true originality" of the literature of the period following World War II (*The Program Era* extends to 2008), McGurl writes early on, "is to be found at the level of its patron institutions, whose presence is everywhere visible in the texts as a kind of watermark" (2009, 4). The institution already complicates the question of creativity, and more recent work, which I will discuss in more detail below, by scholars pursuing the gestation of single books (for instance Clayton Childress in *Under the Cover* (2017) or Alváro Santana-Acuña in *Ascent to Glory* (2020)) or wider questions about publishing (for instance Dan Sinykin in *Big Fiction*) add to the difficulty. The question of where, if anywhere, creativity makes its impact felt is one aspect of this, but as important to me is the question of where in literary studies figures creativity resides, what its value is, and how we relate our work to the knowledge that institutional literary studies has brought forward.

I keep insisting on the term "creativity" here not just because of the way it allows me to trace a through line from the presumption of creativity in AI Go programs through its centrality for literature as "creative" writing, but also because it has lately become a touchstone for literary studies again. Mark McGurl's invocation, for instance, of "craft" as the institution's mediation of authorial experience and creativity finds echoes in Jonathan Kramnick's discussion of creativity in literary scholarship in *Criticism and Truth* (2022), where Kramnick argues that we should understand literary studies as a creative craft—as do Dan Sinykin and Johanna Winant in their recent *Close Reading for the 21st Century* (2025). John Guillory, in both *Professing Criticism* (2022) and *On Close Reading* (2024), likewise foregrounds the way in which literary studies creativity is key to understanding its work. Both participate in a wider debate that cannot easily be untied from anxieties about the state and future of the literary studies disciplines—a problematic situation that this little book, too, cannot escape. In fact, I think that it is against the background of anxieties about the work of literary studies that we can best understand the relevance of discussions around genAI. The linkages between craft, creativity, and knowledge that genAI brings to the fore are already present as points of concern within the discipline—but they appear heightened and sharpened against the background of their potential computational reproducibility, their reduction to textuality.

It's probably correct to say, as Lee Sedol does in the *New York Times*: "People used to be in awe of creativity, originality and innovation. But since A.I. came, a lot of that has disappeared" (Wakabashi and Young 2024). We know, of course, and have known for a long time, that the idea of "art" as autonomous and thereby somehow superior, therefore worthy of attention (or: superior, because worthy of attention) by scholars has serious flaws. We know, of course, that the notion of the "artist" as art's creative instance is problematical. From conceptual art to procedural art to mashup art, we are familiar with the fields of artistic production where art-work, work at art, appears to follow mechanical rules, is merely curational, explicitly recombinatorial. Literary sociological approaches have, more recently, highlighted the way in which the production of any work of literary fiction is enmeshed in a diffuse network of agents, all of which may or may not have "creative" input (see also Lanzendörfer and Norrick-Rühl 2020). But at the same time, we've a markedly hard time to let go of the idea of the artist and of the author, of the value and importance of creativity, even of genius, and perhaps as much in our own work as in the works we study. We rarely explicitly avow them (though sometimes, we do), but they linger, we're bound up with them, and it's genAI's apparently total challenge to them that makes our current moment a moment of deep reflection.

What emerges from the clustering of ideas I have just offered is the way recent theory has labored over the question not just of what literary studies' specific expertise is, but also implicitly how literary studies expertise is related to literary creativity. There is an unease here that is mirrored by the moment of genAI, a tension between demystifying sociological interpretations of what both literary writing and literary studies writing actually are versus attempts to return both to the realms of the ineffable. It's this tension that I find most productive below.

This book is written by a run of the mill literary scholar, not an expert in AI—not, i.e., a computational scientist or even a scholar of digital technology, and it may be more for general literary scholars than scholars of genAI literature. I say this realizing that it's likely to be a major argument against it (reviewers have pointed to this admission to suggest the whole project is flawed). The framing of the issue is, principally, one for scholars like me, those without deep technical knowledge or particular institutional investments in genAI or computational literary studies. I'm one of the people whom Katherine Elkins, writing in *PMLA*, enjoins to be in the conversation: "Who if *not* you" (2024, 562), she asks. I might be on the far end of spectrum she is thinking about here, admittedly. But in this connection, I want to briefly but firmly situate my arguments against potential criticism, some of which is the actual criticism I'm just picking up here. The most direct complaints are variations of this: that my concerns are unfounded because genAI will not be writing literature indistinguishable from human writing (I engage some of that criticism below). Artificial *general* intelligence (AGI) might be capable of it (because of its definitional capacity to actually reason), but AGI is impossible. Set aside for now the problem that it's not clear what AGI actually entails (it's often used to simply mean "computers that think like, or better than, humans," but cf. Fletcher 2022). Both of these criticisms miss my larger points. First, that it's by no means clear that we can now spell out the limits of genAI (but also cf. Fletcher 2022). The story which *The MANIAC* tells is instructive: creativity, or at least something that creativity was asserted for, or something which was indistinguishable from creativity, was emergent here, a consequence of a complex system. Second, that the real limits of genAI are less interesting in the context of this book than the threat and promise of its potential, given ongoing discussions around the forms and values of literary studies. (A third counter suggests that the argument that it would take AGI, i.e., AI indistinguishable in all its expressions from humans, is in fact just a variant of the belief in human genius.)

The obverse criticism looks like this: that I am misunderstanding the functioning, the capacities, and the applications of genAI, specifically because I am not an expert in AI, and so miss that even at the current moment, there is much greater specificity to the uses of genAI in literary production than I envisage. In other words: I'm not giving you the full picture, and I'm not giving genAI its due. Again, I would suggest that what matters to me here isn't the details of how genAI functions (though I address some of this in the first chapter, to establish a shared ground for discussion), but the philosophical and theoretical implications of both our most expansive concerns about AI and the still-possible futures of genAI. To say that, say, genAI already is part of marketing fiction, producing outlines for genre novels, or indeed writing satisfying short fiction, or what have you, is no meaningful counter, in my mind, to asking what genAI means to literary studies ways of studying literature.

The thinking which the current moment of genAI requires of us as literary scholars must be about the most expansive claims for genAI futures, even if, now or in that future, these claims turn out to be overblown. Otherwise, we're neither giving the horizon of genAI its due, nor using its opportunity to the fullest. But all that said: you are free to put this book away if you simply don't agree with its premise. So let me spell this out for you again. We are, right now, at a moment where genAI holds much promise and produces a lot of anxiety. In the specific case of literary studies, this anxiety is largely about the discipline's object (and its pedagogies, though I will not cover this issue), which is to say: the ways in which genAI will be a producer of "literature." We do not know in any real sense how the promises and anxieties will play out; but even now, as promises and anxieties, they offer a moment of reflection for literary studies. Because of the specific nature of genAI as a (largely) stochastic text producer, it challenges fundamental assumptions about the discipline of literary studies. Through the moment of genAI, we can read the discipline anew, or if not anew, at least for this moment. And that's what this little book is trying to do.

Before I proceed, though, another couple of caveats. First: below, I will be distinguishing between genAI text production and human text production. I'm fully aware that this is a facile distinction in so far as all genAI text production rests on a huge archive of human-made textual outputs. The distinction I am making below between human and genAI text production is not meant to endorse the theft of this work by large-language model corpora, nor eradicate the human hand in making genAI outputs happen; it's simply a shorthand. Second, I will be using gen"AI" below, even though I am personally convinced that the "intelligence" bit is a problematic misnomer. GenAI is probably in no useful way best called "intelligent"—though it is, as I will say below, usefully understood as "skilled." The distinction is theoretically important—and worth a pun a little while later—but can't be sustained terminologically in a book on genAI, and so I will continue calling these artificially skilled systems genAI, anyway. Understand this, too, as shorthand. Third: there is a variety of ethically extremely questionable issues bound up in the use of genAI beyond data theft (see, for instance, Crawford 2021). These include, but are by no means limited to: the immense usage of resources, especially of energy, involved in using AI; the role of utterly underpaid human evaluators in the training process of genAI models; and others more. I have no desire to minimize these issues, but for the purposes of this book, I beg permission to bracket them.

References

Bender, Emily M., Timnit Gebru, Angelina McMillan-Major, and Shmargaret Shmitchell. 2021. On the Dangers of Stochastic Parrots: Can Language Models Be Too Big?. In *FAccT '21: Proceedings of the 2021 ACM Conference on Fairness, Accountability, and Transparency* (March), 610–623.

Childress, Clayton. 2017. *Under the Cover: The Creation, Production, and Reception of a Novel.* Princeton: Princeton University Press.

Crawford, Kate. (2021). *Atlas of AI: Power, Politics, and the Planetary Costs of Artificial Intelligence.* New Haven: Yale University Press.

Elam, Michelle. 2023. Poetry Will Not Optimize; or, What is Literature to AI. *American Literature* 95 (2): 281–303.

Elkins, Katherine. 2024. A(I) University in Ruins: What Remains in a World with Large Language Models? *PMLA* 139 (3): 559–565.

Evron, Nir, and Roi Tortakovsky, eds. 2024. The AI Revolution: Speculations on Authorship, Pedagogy, and the Future of the Profession. Special Issue of *Poetics Today* 45 (2).

Fletcher, Angus. 2022. Why Computer AI Will Never Do What We Imagine It Can. *Narrative* 30 (1): 114–137.

Guillory, John. 2022. *Professing Criticism: Essays on the Organization of Literary Study*. Chicago: University of Chicago Press.

Guillory, John. 2024. *On Close Reading*. Chicago and London: University of Chicago Press.

Kirschenbaum, Matthew. 2023. Again Theory: A Forum on Language, Meaning, and Intent in the Time of Stochastic Parrots. In *Again Theory: A Forum on Language, Meaning, and Intent in a Time of Stochastic Parrots*, edited by Matthew Kirschenbaum. *Critical Inquiry*, Online.

Kramnick, Johnathan. 2022. *Criticism and Truth*. Chicago: University of Chicago Press.

Labatut, Benjamin. 2023. *The Maniac*. London: Penguin.

Lanzendörfer, Tim, and Corinna Norrick-Rühl, eds. (2020). *The Novel as Network: Forms, Ideas, Commodities*. Basingstoke: Palgrave Macmillan.

McGurl, Mark. 2009. *The Program Era: Postwar Fiction and the Rise of Creative Writing*. Cambridge: Harvard University Press.

Perlow, Seth. 2024. Generative Theories, Pretrained Responses: Large AI Models and the Humanities. *PMLA* 139 (3): 548–522.

Santana-Acuña, Alváro. 2020. *Ascent to Glory: How One Hundred Years of Solitude Was Written and Became a Global Classic*. New York: Columbia University Press.

Sinkyin, Dan, and Johanna Winant, eds. 2025. *Close Reading for the 21st Century*. Princeton: Princeton University Press.

Wakabashi, Daisuke, and Jin yu Young. 2024. Defeated by AI, a Legend in the Board Game Go Warns: Get Ready for What's Next. *New York Times*, July 10. Online.

CHAPTER 2

AI Literature

Abstract This chapter lays out the foundational issues required to discuss practices of literary studies in the age of genAI. It begins by offering a concise history and description of genAI operations, culminating in the question of what it means to talk about "literature" in the age of genAI. It addresses this question from the angle of implicit and explicit judgments of quality bound up in discussions of the genAI writing, and embedded issues around the question of how we actually come to terms with this quality. The chapter explores assertions that genAI will not be able to write "literature" and suggests that this is, at least, a position more revelatory of what we understand literary studies to be than meaningful in terms of an engagement with genAI. The chapter explores the notions of creative genius embedded here, and reflects on it against discussions that are more founded in literary sociology. Discussions around genAI emerge here as restituting a reflexive humanism in the discipline of literary studies that, in the face of genAI, should require fundamental questioning.

Keywords Literary studies • Literary theory • Creativity • Literary sociology • Artificial intelligence • Literature • Genius • Literary quality • Authorship

T. Lanzendörfer, *AI and the Challenge to Literary Studies*,
https://doi.org/10.1007/978-3-032-25526-6_2

In the Swiss writer Charles Lewinsky's 2024 novel *Täuschend Echt*, explicitly co-authored with the genAI frontends ChatGPT and neuroflash, the protagonist, a just-fired advertising copy writer, begins drafting a novel with the help of genAI—leaving to the AI the entirety of the writing process. He absolves himself by suggesting the "the AI has written it, but I made it up." The moment is supposed, it appears, to at least raise the heckles of readers, to suggest that something wrong has happened in the writer's turn to genAI and his insistence, in small caps, that "I AM creative" (2024, 74, my translation). But why? Consider: the artist Jeff Koons, in one of his very first interviews in 1986, told his interviewer a similar story. Asked in how much he was involved in actually making the objects that he sold as his art ("your work," the interviewer says), he replies: "I'm basically the idea person. I'm not physically involved in the production. I don't have the necessary abilities" (Ottman 1986). To some observers, amongst which I include myself, the ideas of many of Koons's works are not, in fact, very interesting at all, though the technical execution, their craft, is (for instance, in the photorealistic paintings of the EasyFun/Ethereal series).

I want to be careful here to note that I do not mean to denigrate the achievement of artists who work purely conceptually, not even Jeff Koons. What I am interested in, instead, is the inadvertent revaluation of the categories of ability and creativity, of idea and execution, of the notions of skill and craft—categories which will emerge more fully as urgent as this book goes on. In Lewinsky's novel, the expected audience reaction (post-genAI's prominence) complicates exactly what Koons would like us to understand as a useful distinction, and a claim about where creativity resides—a claim about what literature and art in fact constitutively are. This distinction, as I will argue in the following, is at the heart of discussions of genAI literature, and, by extension, of genAI literary studies.

I start this chapter with a very short survey on genAI, with a narrow focus. I begin with a short prehistory to situate our genAI moment in a longer-term trajectory of the workings and meaning of AI. I outline, very briefly, the situation with genAI we're in right now. I concentrate there on the training of genAI programs on large datasets and their at heart stochastic manipulation of training data into recognizable and plausible textual outputs. Such a limning of genAI's functioning is clearly and obviously reductive, but I don't think it is impermissible for my purposes here. Finally, I situate the discussions around the question of what this means as far as the writing of literature is concerned against other contemporary discussions of the meaning of literature, especially in sociological and institutional literary studies—but also beyond. The point of this chapter is, first, to acquaint those of you who are not familiar with the very basics required to follow my argument, and second to begin sketching the relationship between our understanding of what literature is and does to my central point, namely, the work of literary studies in the face of genAI. To understand how contemporary, large language model generative AI functions is relevant for that purpose in order to highlight, again, the significantly changed situation in which we find ourselves. What's new in the genAI moment is not the idea to have computers write texts: it's that suddenly, it works.

Writing with computers, to put it most broadly, is an enterprise of long standing, with the first quasi-successful efforts dating back at least to the 1950s, when the computer scientist Christopher Strachey wrote a program that generated "Love Letters," the first instance of "literary writing produced by the procedural operations of the computer" (Rettberg 2019, 32). As Lillian-Yvonne Bertram and Nick Montfort show, versions of computer-generated text encompass a great variety of genres. They have been produced without letup since that first attempt at a letter (2024).[1] And if it might easily seem to be a very tangential field for employing computation, this writing of literature, in fact it occupies quite a central place in some aspects, the most important of which is language use. At least since 1950, when the computer scientist Alan Turing formulated his famed "Turing test," language use has been a key element in the determination of whether or not something can said to be "intelligent." Turing's point was that if during a chat session, purely textual, you cannot determine if your interlocutor is a human or a computer, then it makes sense to say the computer has exhibited human-level intelligence (Turing 1950). It's easy to misunderstand Turing's test (see, for instance, Wooldridge 2020, 23–25; cf. also Feige 2025)—and not just in the comparatively innocent days of the 1950s and 1960s, when AI's limits were initially being probed. Even before the ChatGPT-craze, in mid-2022, for instance, a Google AI engineer suggested that Google's LaMDA model had become sentient—all on the basis of textual interactions with it (De Cosmo 2022).

[1] There's a second aspect to the connection between computing and literature: Rebecca Roach attends to the overlap of programming and writing literature in the careers of several notable writers and critics of the mid-twentieth century, noting how crucial questions about the nature of literature emerge from its alleged kinship with programming (2025).

Whether or not LaMDA is sentient, of course, that textual information will be all we get. Rather than claiming the computer "is" intelligent, Turing only suggests that it makes no real sense to distinguish between the "real" and the "artificial" in this case—or, perhaps more strongly put, that, judging from outputs alone, we have no means to tell intelligence from the emulation of intelligence.

The question of whether, and what kind, of language use tells us what, if anything, about the language user is obviously central to the contemporary moment of genAI, whose major development is precisely the processing of natural language—of managing "prompts," whether the output to be generated is an image, a video, or itself a text. Literature, from this perspective, emerges as a special problem in the more general issue of natural language understanding, one of the key capabilities that AI researchers have traditionally been after (Wooldridge 2020, 42). The "history of artificial intelligence (AI) is about the history of our understanding of language and meaning," suggests Michael Marcinkowski (2024, 113). For much of the early history of AI development, most effort was expended on "trying to model the *mind*," as Michael Wooldridge has it (2020, 33), through symbolic AI. At least since the 1980s, it has been habitual to contrast this with a "connectionist" approach based on neural networks. Hubert and Stuart Dreyfus offered a number of descriptions of the difference between the two, but perhaps the two most useful for my purposes here are these: symbolic systems modelled intelligence as "problem solving" and "logic"; the connectionist approach, instantiated by research into neural networks, took "learning" and "statistics" (1988, 16). Neural networks emerged virtually at the same time as symbolic AI, in the 1950s—they are not a new idea. But for a number of reasons it does not pay to go into here (see Wooldridge 2020 and Pasquinelli 2023 for different versions of that history), neural networks didn't really catch on in a big way until the 2000s, when, utilizing new "deep" machine learning techniques enabled by more raw computing power and access to vast amounts of data, they bounded forward. One example of a deep learning neural network is AlphaGo, which we have already encountered: a program which used different kinds of learning techniques (including human, expert-level game data) to succeed at becoming the strongest Go player ever. AlphaGo is a combination of two neural networks, called the "judgment" (sometimes "policy") and "value" networks that perform two distinct tasks in the game of Go. The first, in simple terms, picks good moves, one after the other, based on its vast database of human and self-generated games. The second, by contrast, estimates winning chances based on the existing board position. Together, these two networks enable the engine to decide quickly on viable move choices without having to pursue every potential continuation of the game—some, basically, fall out of consideration simply by leading to board positions that can be excluded because they are less likely to lead to success. (I will return below to the implications of the naming convention.)

Despite its technical refinements, in at least one sense this is still brute-force computing: it is made possible by advances in computer technology as much as by thinking about how to frame the job. Today's genAI—the kinds of programs which we are now familiar with in use, the ones that are the core concern for this book, from ChatGPT to LLaMA to Claude—are all programs of this kind, and work thanks to raw computing (and electric) power. They are—this is what the acronym GPT stands for—generative pre-trained transformers, a kind of large-language model neural network used for natural language processing. You presumably already know how these programs function in principle: you communicate your desires to them in a so-called "prompt" that you write, say, in English (this is why it's called "natural language," rather than, say, programming language—philosophers might quibble about what's "natural" about either). The prompt is used by the program to propel the generation of an output that is "new" (thus, it is "generative"), rather than just, say, finding a suitable source for you (as in a web search). In between these two steps, prompting and output, the transformer model undertakes a complex probability calculation based on next token prediction (though cf. Grankowski et al. 2024, and Lindsey et al. 2025). Rather than operating on the basis of words, these tokens are sub-word returning features of language (think "gh" or "ing"). Drawing on a staggering amount of training data (essentially: the Internet and whatever you can find on it), human-driven fine tuning, reinforced learning (of the kind a Captcha has you doing when you find the motorcycle in a segmented image), and millions of previous iterative attempts at creating useful textual output, genAI combines its tokens in, very generally speaking, the most likely way. These outputs and their likelihood can be tweaked. For instance, the "temperature" feature of several models allows users to increase the randomness of outputs, a feature notably often referenced in discussions of AI creativity (see Davis et al. 2024). Because these models are stochastic, they do not necessarily generate correct outputs, as is well known. GenAI produces phantom facts and makes up supporting evidence, a process often called "hallucinations" (see, inter alia, Dziri et al. 2022), because it is not, in fact, checking facts: it outputs sequential token predictions that achieve high degrees of plausibility for the recipient, you. When I speak of genAI above and in the following, these are the operations I envisage occurring in the black box between the prompt and the output.

With that baseline established, I think we can turn to the questions that follow from recognizing genAI's success at making plausible text. We are all, no doubt, well aware of the anxieties the undoubted success of these genAI endeavors in producing text, images, audio, and video has already generated. I'm not going to say much about those anxieties. What I'm more interested in is a question that, admittedly, looks subsidiary to ChatGPT's use by cheating students, politicians faking ethnic audiences through MidJourney, the currently horrifying prospects of Sora 2, troll farms suggesting alternative realities to TikTok users via Runway, or Google engineers handwringing hitting the off button on their PC for fear of murdering a conscious being. I'm interested here in a simpler question, namely, the uses and quality of genAI outputs and their relation to the question of making literature.

The question of whether anything that can be called literature can possibly emerge from the algorithmic processes outlined above for large-language model genAI is bound up in at least two complex problematics. The first is, of course, the workings of genAI that I've just discussed; the second is the question of what it means to call anything "literature" in the first place. "AI Literature" has, already, engaged a wide variety of scholarship. Questions abound: can genAI produce literature? What would it mean to say it produces literature? Answers to these questions, predictably, vary, from Angus Fletcher's straightforward (and repeated) insistence that computers will never write good literature (2021, 2022, 2024), to suggestions that it may already have (Winterson 2025), to the more hedging, careful, and concept-bending suggestions that involve reframing what it would mean to call something "literature" in the first place. The question is also implicit in the frequent discussions of whether genAI can be called an "author," whether or not, and in what ways, it is "creative," and so on. I'd like to start a bit more naively. In important ways, the question of whether AI can produce "literature" has been answered in the affirmative already. We know that ChatGPT has found a role in some contexts that are, broadly and increasingly also more narrowly, literary. Authors in genre fiction, especially in direct publishing on platforms such as KDP, already use it for work such as plotting, developing character backgrounds, to brainstorm new ideas, and so on; in these contexts, it seems that it is doing just fine. We know that readers find it difficult to differentiate genAI poetry from human-written poetry (Porter and Machery 2024); they also find it impossible to differentiate at least short prose texts written by genAI from human-written prose, when the genAI output is generated based on training on a writer's corpus (Chakrabarty, Ginsburg, and Dhillon 2025). Notable writers such as Jeanette Winterson can endorse the outputs of genAI models as "beautiful and moving." And yet, there is resistance to the idea: as the science fiction author Ted Chiang, by no means a luddite at all, put it in a notable *New Yorker* essay: "Right now, the fiction generated by large-language models like ChatGPT is terrible" (2024).

This is the angle I am most interested in—though not so much because I am interested in determining what "good" or "terrible" literature might be. The question that strikes me as most relevant to the concern of this book—namely, what are the consequences of genAI's possible futures for literary studies—is not whether or not genAI actually writes, or whether if it writes, it writes in any allegedly objective way "well"; nor whether it "is" an author, either, or whether or not it "is" creative. What matters is the way we frame our reactions: What does it mean to *say* genAI writes "good" or indeed "terrible" fiction? What are the senses here of good and terrible? And what does it mean to place these evaluative markers so central as categories in the discussion of genAI—why is it important to talk about them, and why are we talking about this old issue of "good" literature at all? Like many of the other terms and categories I will be discussing here, I think the moment of genAI gives us, as literary scholars, a useful occasion to rethink our relation to these terms in a wider sense. In the particular case of genAI, I might suggest they are ill-suited to the actual questions at hand, because they are already bound-up in larger structures of thought from which it will be impossible to divorce them. But I wager the issue is a tad more complicated. The insistence on "good" and "terrible" as descriptive of genAI output is illustrative of the way we tend to bracket these terms as disciplinary concerns otherwise—of our lack of engagement with what it means to think of something as "terrible fiction," or as "good fiction," of the role of judgment in our work and the limits to judgment. At the same time it is also clearly the case that these terms do, in fact, bound off the reach of literary studies. We might come to conclude on the back of discussions around genAI that they are in fact also potentially ill-suited to the concerns of literary studies writ large.

Chiang, in fact, puts the question that is at the heart of discussion very bluntly and more concretely a little while on in his essay when he asks: "Could programs get better than humans at writing fiction in the same way that calculators are better at addition and subtraction." In one sense, we can easily answer "no" to the question, namely, when we focus on "in the same way." Additions and subtractions after all have a simple structure of quality, the binary of "wrong" and "right" plus speed, where speed only matters, though, if the answer is right. Does the computer get 456 + 232.5 more quickly than you, and is it correct?[2] Then it's "better" at addition. This is also generally the way we familiarly understand AI to be better at some things than we are. It's obviously easy to tell when the computer becomes "better" at, say, the game of Go than humans: it's when humans lose. But any answer to the first bit of the question, "could programs get better than humans at writing fiction," rests firmly on the issues of judgment and value bound up in the word "better" or the "terrible" things it seems to do now. What does it mean to be "better at writing fiction"? For Chiang, there is an ineffable linkage between "good" writing and simply being human. He suggests that "any writing that deserves your attention as a reader is the result of effort expended by the person who wrote it"; that it's really vital he is "making choices at every scale"; that it's "heartfelt rather than being eloquent"; that the "experience of subjective feeling and of wanting to communicate that feeling" is vital. In simplest terms, then, "being human" is a necessary (though not sufficient) precondition to making good literature.[3]

Questions around the nature of "good" writing, of what "literature" is, have engaged the discipline basically forever, whether in the form of assertive and declarative judgment, as (very much among others) in F.R. Leavis's *The Great Tradition* (1948), Harold Bloom's late insistence on the Western canon, or indeed the more wide-ranging and iconoclastic choices of poetry undertaken by I.A. Richards for his courses in *Practical Criticism*

[2] It's tangentially relevant to point out here that in a recent study on the transformer model Claude, researchers discovered that Claude, while it will output the information that it has done a mathematical calculation to find the answer to the addition "36+59," in fact undertook a complex search of its textual training data to interpolate the correct solution (95, if you must know). In other words, it still (albeit complexly) arrived at the addition's solution stochastically (Lindsey et al. 2025).

[3] I'm also reminded of Stanley Cavell's question—as an ordinary language philosopher, he may be said to have an outsize but as yet underthought position in genAI discussions—"when is not doing a thing well not doing a thing at all" (2009, 27)?

(1929). (Recent efforts at revitalizing "judgment" as a core concept for future literary studies work, of which more below, fall into the same category.) Against these tendencies, it will seem trite to note that literary studies has, for a very long time now, understood that "literature" is barely a concept. It is a social category, historically grown, and, as Robert Eaglestone notes, "more a verb than a noun" (2019, 5), more a question of what you do with a text than what it might "be."[4] In the famous, Literary Theory 101 definition by Terry Eagleton, literature "in the sense of a set of works of assured and unalterable value distinguished by certain shared inherent properties, does not exist" (2008, 9).[5] It's no surprise whatever, I think, that what Raymond Williams wrote about must sound diagnostically familiar today: the term literature is "often invoked in retrospective, nostalgic, or reactionary moods, as a form of opposition to what is correctly seen as a new phase of civilization" (1977, 54). There is a somewhat odd "reinvestment in origins," in Matthew Kirschenbaum and Rita Raley's phrase (2024, 7), in the gestures toward human creativity, genius, and the questions about genAI's capacity to make literature—precisely through the investment of literature with quality, genius, and in positioning it against genAI's outputs through those innate but largely contentless qualities.

And, of course, the solution which Chiang offers—as we'll see, he's not alone—simply begs the question. Sure: if making good literature requires being human, then genAI won't make good literature. Tautological, but true. But (and here's the rub that will follow us through the rest of the argument I'm making) how would you know? The entire argument here rests on your knowledge of a particular text's authorship, unless you want to argue that "heartfeltness" or "having made choices" or the fact that "effort has been expended" are all *textual* qualities. In this sense, questions of genAI's mind simply do not obtrude. We do not have, with N. Katherine Hayles, to sit disbelievingly before a chat program's output questioning whether it could be "lacking in meaning for the program" (2022, 661). What we're faced with is, in terms of genAI's capacities,

[4] One recent, sociologically informed version of the overarching question of what makes "literature" "literary" is in Leypoldt (2025).

[5] Hannes Bajohr, in a similar phrasing, suggests that "Literature does not exist" (2023, 126, my translation of "Literatur gibt es nicht"—DeepL suggests "There is no literature."). But that's too narrow compared to Eagleton, in either translation, because there clearly is a powerful social category that, perhaps, has no material ontological qualities, but nonetheless, exists.

simpler: its textual output, as in a Turing test, is all we get, and it has its textual properties no matter its creative process. In literary studies terms, it's more complex: suggesting mind behind genAI, after all, answers the question of meaning in analogy to human-written text. Asking after the meaning of text absent mind, by contrast, returns us to the fundamental problems of the discipline itself. GenAI poses this central challenge to us: if we did not know a text was written by genAI, would we be able to tell? And if we think we are *now* able to tell, would we be willing to bet we will be able to tell in the future? And if we do not feel we will always be able to tell genAI and human textual production apart without knowing its origins, what do we think literature even is anymore? Perhaps strikingly, that's probably a basically uninteresting question except for its ramifications for literary study. Most actual readers will know exactly as little about the author A.S. Byatt as they would about a potential "A.I." Byatt; they would instead find themselves recurring to their reading of the text, and whether or not the text plausibly emulated (felt like it had) "heartfeltness," "effort," or "subjective experience."

It makes at least superficial sense, then, to focus on an attempt to deconstruct textuality. Charles Altieri does exactly this when he turns his scholarly attention to two "Shakespearian" poems he has prompted ChatGPT to produce—poems Altieri considers "less than mediocre" (2024, 207). "Good poets," says Altieri, "reject or modify" precisely those "general patterns within the information" that genAI (re-)generates. GenAI, says Altieri, produces "conventionality of diction, flat regularity of meter, [a] lack of personality for the first person speaker, the inability to give a sense of the pleasure in the choices the poet is making, and the failure to distinguish between generalized talk about love or about pain and the actual intense experience of a speaker structurally intensifying and complicating the activity of engaging a beloved" (208). This, he is at pains to note, is not just a question of reproducing Shakespeare: the qualities he's looking for are "in virtually all poetry that engages trained readers."[6]

I quote Altieri here at length because his categories of quality are clearly unexceptional—as literary critics, we might be inclined to subscribe to them. They are nonetheless merely revelatory of the problem we're

[6] I want to note, too, that Altieri appears to assert precisely what I've quibbled with in Chiang: namely, that he can read from, or in the text, the effort of the writer, or better, he appears to allege that he can read from Shakespeare's poetry the "pleasure in the choices the poet is making." I mean, sure?

actually facing. The evaluative judgment the "trained reader" Altieri here undertakes is fraught because it presumes, rather than explicates or justifies, the categories on which it asserts quality—and also presumes, rather than explicates, why, and what it means that, the genAI "sonnet modelled on Shakespeare 128" has "obvious defects" (208). Obvious to whom? And on what grounds? "Are we sure," ask Matthew Kirschenbaum and Rita Raley, correctly, "we know what 'good' output actually is" (2024, 8)? Altieri, speaking for the "trained reader," asserts Shakespeare's poem is better because of its "complexity," "intricacy," "passion," "wit," its capacity to be "concrete" and its "intensity," as against the genAI product's "generalized love" (210), for instance. This "better" is complexly embedded, of course, in thinking about the uses of literature, and specifically of *literature* as an ideological construct, usually drawn on to dismiss more popular mass genres, now mobilized to dismiss the output of genAI. In other words, Altieri uses the opportunity of genAI to postulate exactly that kind of work of "unalterable value" that literary theory has long since (and, to my mind, rightly) dismissed; or, perhaps more likely, he is forced to retire to a position of judgment, with all its inherent problems, because of the challenge of genAI literary production to the field of literary studies that would otherwise emerge. Altieri can in fact be no more sure than anybody else that he knows what good output actually is; and yet, he obviously "knows."

Does it even bear saying, though, that rather than showing a lack of quality, broadly understood, Altieri's point argues for what counts as quality, based on the literature we used to produce and have canonized? Despite and because of Altieri's training, and despite his assurance that he detects all these things in Shakespeare's poetry, his detection of "intricacy," "wit," or "complexity" in Shakespeare's poems is conditioned by his expectation to find them, and also the willingness to ascribe them to text that, in a different context, might just be considered odd. Altieri, you, and I may come to intersubjective agreement that Shakespeare's poetry is "complex." And yet that begs the question of whether, and why, complexity is "good," and whether or not this "good" is free of contexts such as mood, audience, purpose, and so on. It also does not address questions we might, were it not Shakespeare we're discussing, address. Is it complex, or simply overwrought? Where's the tipping point? When is wit just a dad joke addressed to other dads? If "intricacy" is good, is "dense" also good? When does the one become the other? Does anybody know what any of these words *mean*?

I don't mean to be too facile or flippant here. But it does bear pointing out the place of Shakespeare's poetry in the larger literary landscape, and the question which goes undiscussed in both Altieri and Chiang: namely, what the point of literary quality that only trained readers can detect actually is. In one, widely-reported, November 2024 study, audiences confronted with the demand to decide whether any particular poem was written by a human or modelled "after" a human author by gen AI were unable to distinguish with any degree of confidence—"participants' answers differed only slightly from chance," and where they did differ, the study's authors conclude, they did so on the basis of shared, but flawed, heuristics (Porter and Machery 2024, 3). When asked to judge the quality of these poems, genAI poetry was rated higher than human writing in 13 of 14 categories. These categories range from the formal ("rhythm") to the emotional ("inspiring") and included a general "overall quality." The only category in which no statistical difference could be detected in readers' evaluations was "originality"—but even there, human authors held genAI only to a draw (4–5). And what's more: this barely even needed pointing out. As Hannes Bajohr recounts, when one of the very first German stochastic poems was printed in a magazine, readers were completely divided over its aesthetic merit—in 1960 (see Bajohr 2024, 336). There's a reason why Rupi Kaur is a best-selling poet, but virtually unread in the academy (see Baßler 2021): the categories by which we measure "quality" are not popular in the first place. GenAI sets this into starker relief, I think. "The semantic choice to not call computer-generated texts 'literature' is of more value to authors than it is to readers," suggests Leah Henricksen. That is certainly the case, but it is more than a semantic choice—it is also a recognition of the system of valuation we are currently working with. Henricksen herself, after all, distinguishes in her essay between "genre literature" that "may be more easily computer-generated," even to the extent of being "eventually indistinguishable from a human-written one" (2024, 294). Capital-L Literature, in this version as in Altieri's, appears to be prima facie excluded from the realm of possibility.

I don't want to overemphasize the point, by any means. But consider the relevance here, perhaps, of genAI models that are trained in such a fashion as to produce "winsome nonsense words" (Kraus 2023) rather than semantically recognizable ones (one possibility clearly enabled by genAI's prediction of subword tokens, rather than word-size tokens). The results, says Kari Kraus, is "not unlike Lewis Carroll's *jabberwocky*" or, we might say, some of the play with phonetics in James Joyce. Which is not to say that these programs "write like James Joyce," only to point out that it's difficult to judge what kinds of modifications of the "conventional patterns of information," to return to Altieri, should count for literary innovation—or how we would speak about them, if we encountered them in the wild.

It's perhaps not saying too much that the example of William Shakespeare simply poisons the well. Symptomatically, it asserts an utterly impossible standard, one impossible to match (by dint of general acclamation) even by other humans, even as it suggests that standard's independence from historically, culturally, and disciplinarily specific criteria of judgment that themselves tend to remain underexplained. In this drawing of genAI textual production into the regime of valuation, of course, contemporary literary criticism is just exercising a move that has become more familiar over the past decade or so, even for human-written texts. Seth Perlow argues that on the assumption that genAI has made it "easy to generate coherent texts of any length in any familiar genre," while "the issue of quantity [is] rendered moot, that of quality remains" (2024, 550). I'm not sure myself what the "issue of quantity" has been (I don't think there's a dearth of fiction writing out there, even of "good" literature), but the notion that genAI returns us to the question of aesthetics as our field's future calling—evaluative aesthetics, saying what "better" means—has taken what is at first glance a somewhat surprising foothold. Reactions to genAI's textual production have overtly returned us to the kind of "strenuous aesthetic appreciation" which Mark McGurl, in the conclusion to his *The Program Era*, suggested would make us sound "goofily anachronistic" (2009, 409). It clearly no longer does. Critics besides Altieri, though usually without his willingness to commit to concrete terms for "good," are calling explicitly for it because of genAI: "the rise of LLMs should further motivate the already decades-old return to aesthetic judgment of value" (Perlow 2024, 550). This demand can also echo through subtle redefinitions, as when Katherine Elkins suggests that the new genAI outputs require "the kind of careful qualitative work of close reading that we excel at," which soon morphs into "qualitative assessment" (2024, 560). The initial "qualitative" can be understood without the overtones of good or bad, but the second, again, ties close readings to judgments—here, of ethics. Chiang, i.e., is in good company when he worries about the quality of genAI outputs: academics do so too. In our case, though, the issue is slightly different. As a reader, and even as a reviewer, Chiang, of course, is well within his ambit to judge writing on a simple scale of "good" to "terrible," by criteria either of his own devising or socially sanctioned. In fact, this is exactly what happens in the case of Jeanette Winterson's public blessing of OpenAI's short story "A Machine-Shaped Hand" as "beautiful and moving" (2025)—it's good, because it moves her.[7] As literary scholars/critics, we have habitually not been forced to do the same. The decision what it is worth engaging with has generally been made for us: we read and interpret books by authors that are published as and ideally also widely recognized as literary writers, texts drawn from canons of important work. Quite a lot hinges, in fact, on the distinction we can draw between those who explicate importance through interpretative engagement (us) and those who give opinions of quality by reference to only allegedly intersubjective measures (*New York Times* reviewers, say—but also the ordinary readers who post on GoodReads and simply can state which books they like).

And yet, the return to judgment makes some sense as a response to genAI. That does not mean it is correct as a response, and not just as a response to genAI, but to the plight of the humanities generally. I think it makes sense as a response at first glance because, as Michael Clune puts it, "artistic judgment has the structure of a skill" (2019, 181). I will be talking in more detail below about how, in current thinking about literary studies practices, "skill" has come to the forefront and why. For now, let me suggest that the invocation of a skill appears to seek to shield both literature and literary studies professors from the encroachment of genAI without forcing us to reflect on the fundamental challenge that genAI poses—it allows us to sidestep the issue by returning us to an earlier state of the field in which we ruled supreme. I do not think that the challenge of genAI literary production will be that it returns us to make aesthetic judgments central to our work. Instead, it forces us to consider categorical assumptions about these kinds of judgments that have become so habitual as to not have required consideration for a long time. We turn to the question of aesthetic judgment because it appears as though here is an opportunity to either categorically bound of human writing from genAI writing

[7] There's much to say about Winterson's short essay that goes beyond the point of this book, but I do want to note her impressive line: "Machines do not feel, but they can be taught what feeling feels like." I'm reminded of the robot Bender B. Rodriguez's line from the animated sitcom *Futurama*: "Being a robot's great. But we don't have emotions, and sometimes that makes me feel very sad" (S04E11, "Anthology of Interest II.") An actually meaningful re-writing of Winterson's line would suggest: machines do not feel, but they can be made to write what feeling reads like.

(as in the case of Chiang and Altieri and Fletcher, below) or, at least, permit some space for human work (as in Perlow).

I need to return to the issue of judgment as a response to genAI literary writing below in the context of genAI literary studies, but it is quite necessary now to also cover some of the other bases on which contemporary criticism has rejected the idea that genAI textual outputs are qualitatively similar to human writing. Altieri and others suggest that genAI fails to generate literature (implied by the notion of the "good") because its textual work fails poetically, unable to emulate the peculiar ways in which "good" poetry makes language work (see also Elam 2023). Other critics have suggested that even narratively, genAI cannot do the work that would be required to produce literature.

Despite its conceptual differences, especially its focus on the technical capacities of the software-hardware combination of the computer as such, Angus Fletcher's insistent point that AI will never produce narrative, on account of computers' fundamentally different "thought" processes, is still a relative of the points already discussed. Fletcher's major assertion is, I think, a technological echo of the above arguments insisting on essential human features in creativity. He suggests that while brains think narratively (see also Breithaupt 2023), computers calculate logically, and that logic and narrative (and implicitly logic and creativity) are irreconcilably different operations. Most vitally, I think, he suggests that we should not expect the computer's logics to reproduce (except by non-narrative means) narrative through logic: "because narrative is a process" itself, and "you can't have a different process of doing the same process" (Fletcher 2022, 119). Because the computer's calculations cannot be narrative, its outcomes cannot be narratives, either. But what about the belief, and the claims, raised by Winterson and OpenAI—that genAI already in fact has written not just any, but a *good* short story—and so, a narrative? Fletcher's objection would be to say that what genAI has done here is to generate "swap-pits that have been cherry picked by humans and assisted by readerly generosity to create the illusion of [a] short story" (2022, 130).[8] My own point, to reiterate, is: how would you know this textually? And this could be expanded to ask: so what? What about the illusion of a short story is worse than a short story?

[8] This is also the argument that Emily Bender et al. (2021) offer, and it's reminiscent of the larger argument which Steven Knapp and Walter Benn Michaels have been pursuing for forty years now (1982, 2023). I have more to say about this argument in the third section.

The question is not whether computers can think narratively, as Fletcher has it; it is whether genAI programs trained on narrative writing can reproduce writing that is narratively plausible enough in its textual outputs, to as near an approximation of Shakespeare (if you like) as is possible. The question there, basically, is whether or not the textual itself encodes narrative thinking, or perhaps more properly, if the narrative-textual itself is impossible to produce without narrative thinking. Fletcher asserts yes—but can do so only by suggesting that readers reading stochastic-logical texts as narrative are duped into thinking they've read a story when they've actually not. The question is whether the need to understand causality, and to be able to integrate causal connections into logic processing, is a prerequisite to output a text that looks causal (or, for that matter, like it's imbued with "feeling")—the same question, essentially, that Hannes Bajohr formulates in his afterword to his novel *(Berlin, Miami)*. Here, Bajohr suggests that its lack of ability to answer the crucial question of plot—"why?" that is a challenge for genAI. If "cause and effect" are impossible to "teach" a genAI, argues Bajohr, then all we can hope for are "correlation texts," "surface narrations" (2023, 247, my translation). He reinforces this point a little later: a "large-language model can only simulate any causality through correlations" (255).[9] But ultimately, Bajohr also concludes that it is the "moment of reading that gives a text meaning," suggesting that "in reality, the distinction between correlation and causality is possibly not that important"

[9]Without meaning to harp too much on it, this line of argument appears to be at least somewhat confused. Bajohr's point, like Fletcher's, appears to be that in human-made text, the specific textual output is arrived at causally, i.e., the text is there because of a human agent's choices in the arrangement of the text. "Causality" here cannot mean merely that these textual outputs are there because someone pressed a key on a keyboard, because this kind of mechanical causality is clearly also available to genAI (the textual outputs is there because an algorithm generated a stochastic output). Causality can also not mean that the text's content exhibits causality; in text, all causalities are, after all, only fictions of causality. The queen did not "causally" die of grief, if you like, except in the textual illusion. So the "why" in Bajohr's argument initially does not emerge textually at all, it is put into the text by a human—human intelligence, human decision making has caused the chain of events that produce the text (including the pressing of keys). But not only will we see, below, that authors frequently dispute this causal link themselves; it also makes no sense, as before, to separate out an ineffable cause and its textual consequences from the textual consequences of mere correlation, or indeed of chance. In Fletcher and Bajor both, it seems that causality is simply another way of describing authorial intention.

(266).[10] Bajohr's point is an important one for my purposes, because it suggests that today, post genAI, the distinction between causality and correlation is indeed a textual property. He does not spell this argument out, but it follows from his suggestion early on that the inability of producing causal relations outside of correlation is the source of "productive mistakes" through which "causality appears as in a Fata Morgana" and a "never quite succeeding" narration of the "why" (247). GenAI texts currently bear the traces of this—though perhaps more so in the longest form of the novel than in shorter narrative forms that enthused Winterson, and, of course, not in non-narrative texts.[11]

That the emulation of a certain quality (standing in for the production of quality as such?) is a thing suggested by a somewhat famous, repeated, point made by the TV producer Aaron Sorkin (*The West Wing*, *The Newsroom*) about his own writing. Sorkin claimed repeatedly that it has "the sound of intelligence. I can imitate that sound, but it is not organic. It's not intelligence. It's my phonetic ability to imitate the sound of intelligence" (in Harris 2012)—television's very own Turing-type test. And AIron Sorkin is unsurprisingly equally adept at this. As Fletcher has it, genAIs are "playing a game, the purpose of which is to dupe us into thinking that we're reading something intellectually coherent" (2022, 127).[12] The issue of intellectual coherence's actual presence will engage me more fully in the next section; for now, I want to merely reiterate that all this hinges, in the final analysis, on knowledge that goes

[10] There is a suggestive link here, I think, in this sense of causality and correlation, to the way we narrativize our own lives. Our own life stories take on the guise of the „illusion of a story, "too, in the way that we tend to reduce to causality („I studied X because Y") what, in actuality, must have been a vastly overdetermined, finally utterly opaque—I'm tempted to say: black boxed?—process. I return to this point below when I look at the narrativization of the creative process.

[11] In a fascinating experiment, the novelist Tom Comitta's *People's Choice Literature: The Most Wanted & Unwanted Novels* (Columbia UP, 2025) is based on a survey of readers' desires for a "novel just for you" (13), respondents' concrete requests, and the support of OpenAI's Playground LLM (20). The result were two novels: one, a fairly readable though entirely unexceptional thriller; the other, a complicated, virtually unreadable "literary" novel. Here as elsewhere in the current ecosystem of genAI, prompting well, and entering into what Comitta calls a "dialogue" with the LLM, were key in developing the actual novel.

[12] There is some weirdness going on here and elsewhere in Fletcher's writing with the anthropomorphization of genAI. Note, too, the way in which here again as elsewhere in Fletcher's argument, genAI is at least rhetorically ascribed intention, which should have the kinds of consequences for reading practices that I describe in the following section.

beyond the merely textual. To successfully imitate good fiction is to be good fiction.[13]

This is also why I do not want to quibble at all with Fletcher's notion that "literature is more than logic," that it is not just language (129), that its reception involves "emotion, imagination, suspense, and other psychological processes that can be set into motion by words but are biologically independent of language and therefore not reducible to the internal logical properties of a text" (130). My point is rather to highlight the distinction between genAI *literature* (a social category) and genAI *text,* even genAI poetry or genAI fiction more generally, and, specifically, of the difficulty in locating in text anything and all that is that "more" than logic and language. Fletcher's explicit argument is that text is the only prompt readers receive to create narrative, meaning, and so forth in their own minds. But it is also that such narrative-generating text is impossible for genAI to produce. While it's possible to hold both of these things, Fletcher does not in fact show both: rather, he asserts that there are some cases in which the narrative-generating minds of readers are "duped" into thinking they've read a short story, and some cases in which they have actually read a short story—cases which simply track onto the entirely effable inhumanity of genAI and the ineffable humanity of real literature.[14]

But, of course, this only brings us back to square one, the moment where we discovered that the basic assumption underlying most discussions of the relative quality and the relative capacity of genAI and human literary producers boiled down to the simple and undeniable point that genAI is not human. That, at the beginning of this chapter as here, just begs the question we're after.

The question of whether it takes anything particularly human to make art (whether spiritual, psychological, biological, or otherwise specific to

[13] The pre-history of this entire way of thinking is in Colin Burrow, *Imitating Authors* (2019); here, before the current genAI moment, Burrow already anticipates the possibility that the history of literature *as* imitation already implicates an AI future.

[14] In the context of thinking about the possible futures of genAI, and specifically its disappearance behind its own capacity to emulate human literary writing, an angle that some of the recent discussion has foregrounded disappears into the background: the question of whether or not, and what it would mean that, "AI narratives have the power to radically challenge the way that audiences view the world" (Thorne 2019, 820), for instance, by reframing readers' expectations or offering something like insight into the non-human. This is interesting, but not key to my concerns here, because it's essentially subordinate to the more fundamental issues I want to raise. I note this here for something approaching completeness' sake.

Homo sapiens as a species) is one of long standing, and perhaps most familiar from the mathematico-philosophical (probability) problem of a typing monkey producing, if given an infinite amount of time, all possible books. In a more familiar version, it's a thousand monkeys at a thousand typewriters writing all the works of Shakespeare. In the philosophical problem, the monkeys were "an abstract device that produces an endless random sequence of letters and symbols," as Wikipedia's article phrases it; actual monkeys, as intrepid researchers have since found out, are not actually very inclined to type anything, let alone for an infinite amount of time (see Fletcher 2024). But the more important point here, again *pace* Fletcher, is that genAI shares a lot of similarities with that abstract device, with the twist of not producing text randomly. (Whether that is, in fact, a hindrance or a benefit is by no means clear.)

As I noted in the introduction: we would probably prefer to not think of the production of art as a stochastic exercise. What we would prefer, though, is neither here nor there. Again: genAI either will, or will not, end up capable of producing literary texts that are textually indistinguishable from human writing. I do not know, and neither do you. What emerges from the openness of the question is precisely my concern: namely, the possibility that it does not take human agency to write "good" literature.

As the science fiction writer Theodore Sturgeon famously remarked: 90% of *everything* is crap. If I go to ChatGPT and ask it to "write me brilliant poem," the output will not be Shakespeare. But that's true of humans writing poems, too (except, often, Shakespeare). So, even if we hold with Altieri and Fletcher that "no computer … would ever be Shakespeare" (Fletcher 2024, 126), in the grand scheme of things that's no major concession, for only Shakespeare ever was Shakespeare anyway. Writing Shakespeare is just phenomenally unlikely, even for intelligent, agential human beings. But not only may writing Rupi Kaur be far less so—there will be lots of intermediate steps which will also be far less unlikely, including the majority of the kinds of texts which contemporary literary studies engages as its bread-and-butter. The category of the "literary" carves out a moment of the exceptional from the dross of convention: to ask after the "literary" is already to ask after the lasting, the best, and so on.

In fact, you will recall that the point of this discussion of genAI literature has never been to adjudicate the literariness of genAI textual production. Rather, it has been to highlight how the debates around genAI shine a spotlight on the greater discussions we are having, or should be having, in literary studies about all forms of text explicitly as the output of writing—human included.[15] As John Guillory has put it, "the margin of the creative in [AI's] amalgamation [of human writing] is yet to be determined" (2024, 81). More fundamentally, the "margin of the creative" in human writing has, in the past decade or two, come under increasing scrutiny within literary studies. If the first objection to genAI literature was that it is, generally, not "good" (enough to be considered literature), and the second is that it cannot produce narrative, the third objection is a more broadly philosophical one. It is that genAI is not "creative," where creativity is the hallmark and point of origin of "good" writing. Precisely what creativity is is, and has been for long time, contested, without even addressing the question of stochastic creativity at all.[16] But it is inevitably bound up in the cluster of concerns that has propelled this discussion of genAI literature.

The curious admixture of an understanding of creativity as crucial to the creation of art works, the realization that it is difficult to quantify or even reliably identify, and the struggle to embed it into the larger systems of production and dissemination that in fact make art possible as art can be exemplarily seen in Adam Moss's recent *The Work of Art: How Something Comes from Nothing*. The subtitle already hints at Moss's crucial question: how can—as the back cover has it—"transcendent novels, painting, jokes, movies, songs, and more" come onto the blank slate of the white canvas or empty word processing screen? Moss uses a combination of interview and notes taken by artists in the process of composition to illuminate the creation of a number of well-known works of art, among them Michael Cunningham's novel *The Hours* (1998), Sheila Heti's *How Should a Person Be?* (2010), and George Saunders's *Lincoln in the Bardo* (2017). What emerges from Moss's intensive engagement, alas, is interesting but disappointing. Despite the large number of qualities that his interviewees together list to explain their artistic success, Moss is finally reduced to

[15] I discuss some of the issue of how we relate to literary texts as texts, and how we relate to them as artifacts which require of us a different kind of attention that is often not wholly coherent in Lanzendörfer (forthcoming) and Lanzendörfer (2025).

[16] This is without pointing out, as Samuel W. Franklin has recently done, the complicated history of "creativity" as both a term and a concept, and its arising in particular post-war situation in which "as assorted cluster of academic psychologists, management gurus, advertising executives, and engineers [...] constructed the concept of creativity as we know it today" (2023, 7), including as "a psychological cure for [the] structural and political contradictions of the postwar order" (14)—among them an apparent decline in the importance of the individual in the United States.

suggesting that the answer to art's genesis is couched in mystery. There is "a before and an after," namely, "the acquisition of skills" versus the "practical activity" of making; but between that fore and after is a "mysterious part," a thing that "cannot be put into language" (400). On the one hand—a bit like Altieri and Fletcher's invocation of Shakespeare—the whole project presupposes what it also sets out to show: namely, that the best way of finding out "how something comes from nothing" in art is to foreground the artist, and most importantly, the successful (and thus, already exceptional) artist. On the other, Moss's project explicitly seeks to disentangle the ineffable, the "*miracle*" from "its exact opposite" (2024, 11, original emphasis), "the artist's process in all its mundanity" (12) and fails.

Moss looks into "art making as a solo activity" (13), but more than that. He looks into art as a process. Problematically, here the artist's recollection of that process of making holds the key, requiring, among other things, faith in the idea that artists are capable of recollecting and capable of understanding their process, rather than merely able to retell a plausible story of their process, if you will, to sell the illusion of a life story. What the prose writers in Moss's book finally seem to hit on is a process of self-curation, one in which writing takes on a life of its own. In George Saunders's terms, "sometimes those sections you eject just keep coming back in"; "things that I didn't know the book was going to do, it started doing" (386). In Moss's book, complicated texts emerge from the "solitary act of art making" (404)—even those texts which, like Heti's *How Should a Person Be*, had been made in explicit contact with other artists and even publishers.

Moss's book is illustrative of the dual impulse in discussing artistic creativity to return to the embodiment of that creativity—the author—with a willingness to leave off attempting to more than locate the gap in the experience of creativity. We know where it happens—but not how, or why. And in so far as Moss's book necessarily turns to successful artists, and indeed *artists*, rather than mere writers, it also presupposes that we have more to learn from these exceptional performers of creativity, rather than the more mundane ones.

In their extensive discussion of creativity, Keith N. Sawyer and Danah Henriksen expand on what Moss does in his vignettes: they ask, sustainedly, after the way creativity works, and what it is in the first place—a "surprisingly difficult" thing to do, as they acknowledge (2024, 7). The two definitions they offer are slightly at odds, but usefully so. The "individualist" definition is the one that we've basically encountered above, implicitly and explicitly: "Creativity is a new mental combination that is expressed in the world" (8, original in italics). The sociocultural definition is rather different: "Creativity is the generation of a product that is judged to be novel and also to be appropriate, useful, or valuable by a suitably knowledgeable social group" (9, original in italics). It doesn't take much to parse these two definitions out onto the discussions around genAI: if creativity necessarily is a "mental" combination, then genAI cannot be creative—it (we assume) has no mind. If, on the other hand, creativity is judged from its product, then there's little reason to think prima facie that genAI cannot be creative.[17] But the point here is not just that there are valid definitions of creativity that would include genAI textual production. The point is that there is something meaningful to be said about the choice, prevalent in current literary studies discussions of genAI, to retreat to the individualist position on creativity, something that is symptomatic of the field's current anxieties around its object.

What emerges perhaps most forcefully from Sawyer and Henriksen's volume is that what we have heard above about creativity is, first and foremost, a Western cultural framing of a complex set of processes, most of which do not in fact easily fall into the schema we tend to have for creativity. In their discussion of writing as a creative process, for instance, they note the "Western cultural belief in the authenticity of a writer's output" (2024, 368) which we have already encountered in discussions of genAI. As a useful corrective, Sawyer and Henriksen draw on the familiar story (to literary studies folks) of T.S. Eliot's *The Waste Land* and the editorial interventions made by Ezra Pound to turn Eliot's somewhat sprawling original manuscript into the tight, focused piece that earned Eliot his fame.[18]

[17] In their own discussion of genAI creativity, Sawyer and Henriksen are largely concerned with the question of "who" created any given genAI output—"Who is the author? Who has the creative agency," they ask (328). Here, as above, these questions are no doubt valid but, as I have been at pains to argue, are not key to the question I'm pursuing.

[18] Eliot, as Sawyer and Henriksen point out, acknowledged Pound as "the greater craftsman" in his dedication of *The Waste Land*. The notion here might easily appear a slight dig at Pound's expense, suggesting that Eliot's inspirations required the more down-to-earth handicraft of Pound, without making Pound therefore the greater *poet*. We needn't read it that way in order to see how the notion of craft is important here. "Craft," I will argue further below, becomes a category that can translate the ineffability of creative inspiration into an ostensibly more material register, but without losing the ineffability, the alleged impossibility of ever getting at the exact way this object came into being in this way.

Compared to Eliot, we know very little indeed of Shakespeare's creative process; combined with his status as Western literary culture's acknowledged GOAT, this makes him a very easy pick as a foil for genAI. But he is the wrong foil. We know, of course, that "writers will always work in a sociocultural system, collaborating with members of the field, working with the conventions of the domain" (Sawyer and Henriksen 2024, 379). The more important question may be what we do with that knowledge—beyond ignoring it in favor of the ineffable genius of Shakespeare. The discussions around genAI, paradoxically, have thrown us back here to a version of literary studies that appears willing to ignore literary sociology completely. That we are taking the opportunity of genAI already to spur a discussion of the place of creativity, as the ultimate source for literary quality as well as the source of the quality of literariness, could easily come as a surprise in this context. For a considerable while now, literature has been read as the product not, or at the very least not only, of individual writers, but of a far larger system of literary production with a large number of agents and interests that need to be moderated, consciously or unconsciously, in the production of literary texts.

Mark McGurl's 2009 *The Program Era* is perhaps still the most prominent example of sociological approaches to literary production.[19] The book investigates the role the MFA programs that proliferated at US universities in the wake of World War II had in the production of literary writing and the making of literary writers. "The literature of this period [roughly: 1950 through 2008] would remain obsessed with individuals and their individuality [...] but its true originality, I will argue, is to be found at the level of its patron institutions, whose presence is everywhere visible in the texts as a kind of watermark" (2009, 4). As McGurl notes: "the mythology of scientific creativity is one of inexplicable 'Eureka' moments and, in the arts, of the mysteriously pleasing effluence of unpredictable personalities" (72)—precisely the Western cultural conception that Sawyer and Henriksen also identify. Against this individualist notion of creativity, McGurl throughout his study highlights the complex and complicated relationship between the institution of the MFA program and its collective demands on writers, importantly its focus on a triad of terms

[19] Which is obviously not to say that it is the first, or the most important. We might nod to Macherey (1978), Bourdieu (1996) or Moretti (1998) at the very least, in different registers. But for the purposes of this book, I want to stick with the more recent past.

that is also familiar to us in the context of genAI criticisms: experience, creativity, and craft (103).

McGurl's book, it must be said, obviously does not endorse or even consider the question of creativity absent humanity. Indeed, while he champions "aesthetic-institutional totality" over "individual writers," he does so because it signals to him a fundamentally democratizing "general human creativity" (74). But at the same time, McGurl's book stands centrally for the argument that the kind of simple author-text relation that has implicitly re-emerged in the wake of the genAI challenge is unsustainable, certainly in the contemporary literary field.

In the wake of McGurl's book, literary sociological approaches have also come to study at length concrete instantiations of the social processes of making literature, two of which I want to explore here for their relevance. One discusses the production of a world literature canon classic, Gabriel García Márquez's *One Hundred Years of Solitude*; the other, the making of one of the thousands of literary fiction novels that get published every year, Cornelia Nixon's *Jarrettsville*. Both of these novels are, in so far as they are not genre fiction, clearly "literary" novels. And both, at least according to the literary sociological account, are ill understood as the products of the creativity, the choices of their authors. In Alváro Santana-Acuña's recounting of the writing of *One Hundred Years of Solitude*, the process that made García Márquez's novel is called "networked creativity," the "real force" (2020, 114), an "act of distributed cognition and agency" (132). In Clayton Childress's discussion in *Under the Cover*, the same basic idea is called "the social life of artistic creation" (Childress 2017, 19). Both of these studies suggest that it is by no means easy, if at all possible, to trace textually a novel's creation, or, for that matter, to read from the text the authorial process. Writers, suggests Childress, are "a collective noun" (20) and creativity itself becomes "social collage" (21)—and all this before it even leaves what Childress calls the "field of creation" to enter the "field of production" and finally the "field of reception"; similarly, Santana-Acuña highlights the deeply social nature of all stages of its road to canonicity. *A Hundred Years of Solitude* had to "adapt to the creative conditions set by the New Latin American Novel"; it was written through networked creativity; it had to "comply with the market conditions of the Spanish-language publishing world" and had to be consecrated through the "collaboration, adaptation, and competition among cultural brokers" (2020, 280).

In so decentering the authorial subject, none of these literary sociologists deny the de facto presence of an author, of course. Santana-Acuña's point that García Márquez "changed his literary style to find a balance between economic and rhetorical language" (117) still, obviously, centers the writer's agency. But it already suggests that around that agency cluster aspects of creativity that are not within the remit of the creative subject. García Márquez's network offered him "advice on solving technical problems at the level of ideas, format, and style in his novel" (125); similarly, the writing workshops of the MFA program in McGurl with their feedback loops and the various stages of writing which Cornelia Nixon's novel underwent are a far cry from the kind of romantic artistic autonomy and self-determination that some of the responses to genAI suggest will save literature.

Childress ends his story of the genesis of *Jarrettsville* by suggesting that, "in the crafting of *Jarretsville*, 'Cornelia Nixon' had become a bit of a collective noun; the figurehead undergirded by a long acknowledgements page, and an even longer list of unnamed people who she believed should be acknowledged" (2017, 36). In perhaps the most radical recent revisioning of the process of making literature, Dan Sinykin sets out to "show how much we miss when we fall for the romance of individual genius" (2023, 4)—so much so that, with a barely workable "if," Sinykin acknowledges that "if this book has a villain, it is the romantic author" (25)—exactly the figure which has re-emerged in the genAI discussions. In Sinykin's argument, the best way to read the production of literature is through the "conglomerate superorganism" that produces the "properties" (2023, 12) of the fiction which emerges from it, rather than the individual author (though, it bears pointing out, this radical thesis is considerably weakened over the course of the book). In Sarah Brouillette's summary of Sinykin's argument, "authorship is a product of the system, and the creative genius is a myth to be done away with" (2024, 101), even as Sinykin's prose appears to "preserve idealization of the autonomous author" (102). As in Foucault and Barthes, the author in Sinykin becomes explicitly an epiphenomenon, and unlike in Foucault and Barthes, Sinykin explicitly invokes the specter of genAI in citing the musician Grimes as saying: "'we all kind of function like AI: we're all a product of all the content that we feed ourselves. And so, it's funny to be like, 'Oh, this is my work.' In reality, it's the result of thousands of years of human art making'" (2023, 9). As in much discussion of contemporary genAI, in Sinykin's book, rational analysis sits at odds with idealistic conceptions of literature. Sinykin cannot quite let go of the author as point of origin—partially, one supposes, because it allows him to tell funny stories.

What emerges from this discussion of literary sociology and its decentering of the author-figure for a more careful analysis of the actual process of making contemporary literature (rather than imagining Shakespeare's writing) is the close proximity discussions of genAI literature have to this. Slightly too flippantly: if we hear in contemporary fiction, at least, echoes of the "pleasures of the choices the author is making," to borrow from Charles Altieri, we're just hearing things we would desperately like to hear: authentic voices, lived experience, mediated-unmediated access to other human subjectivities. As the literary sociological approaches make clear—and as we well knew from the countless historical examples of concrete collaborative creation—this has always been a myth. And yet it appears to be a myth we cannot, disciplinarily, fully abandon. It's unsurprising that literature itself has participated in the affirmation of human genius, in what Sarah Brouillette has cuttingly identified as novels preoccupied with producing "an ennobling sign of one's distinct creative intelligence" (2024, 124). It's, after all, a good sales pitch, now more than ever. But even in literary studies, we appear to be stuck with the Kantian idea of genius and the notional centrality of artistic creativity, both of which center the exceptional individual—the kind of individual about whose "works" it is possible to write monographs, who can carry by dint of their name our engagement with their writing.[20] And we're stuck with it even though, in practical terms, we know it's not true: that writing a literary novel, or indeed any kind of fiction, is at the very least a collaborative and sometimes adversarial process, one which involves forms of curation but also forms of outright rejection, purely instrumental acceptance of market logics, inputs of all kinds.

One of the ways the impact from all kinds of agents besides the author herself might be framed is through the idea of curation. Curation selects that is worthwhile, what works, what fits—and has become one of the central watchwords in thinking about how genAI might produce literature. In its need to be curated, genAI is hardly different from human writers. But genAI lacks self-curation, of course—an ability to judge its own output, be displeased by it and rework it. As the interviews in Adam Moss's *The Work of Art* make clear, this is a key feature at least of artist's

[20] Meaningfully, the idea of genius, as the Heinrich Bosse (2014) has pointed out, also legitimizes an author's ownership of a text.

self-reportage of the creative process. One of the few concrete processual things that Adam Moss sees almost across the board in artistic creation is self-curation, the making of decisions as to what works, and what doesn't. As the example of Saunders shows, sometimes even this self-curation is mysterious—whole passages of novels removed, then worming their way back in. But more importantly for my purposes, this act of self-curation is (for given values of what counts as winning in literature) faulty. The example of Eliot is clear here: Eliot's self-curation mechanisms failed him to the extent that he wanted his work to find acceptance with Pound, and to the extent of Pound's beliefs about what would find acceptance with a larger audience. Taking a step back from the concrete, this no doubt holds true more generally: authors insufficiently self-curate for artistic quality in most instances of art-making, elsewise we would be incapable of finding any kind of critical-judgmental purchase (all books would be great). Self-curation eliminates what writers themselves find unhelpful to their texts and keeps what they believe helpful (though see below), not what makes a text, as it were, better or worse, except if you already hold with the notion that it must, because authors are geniuses. And that's before we acknowledge again that acts of deletion through self-curation by definition do not appear in the text, and may very well have made an existing text worse. Who knows what brilliant lines used to be in *Hamlet*?

I described above the two neural networks on which AlphaGo runs its calculations. It's almost certainly too simple to just suggest that the ideas of "value" and "policy" in AlphaGo's algorithms track easily on the ideas of "judgment" and "writing" in literary production, that they are instances of self-curation, but it is nonetheless suggestive. The major difference, of course, is that while computationally very involved indeed, "value" is ultimately a simple idea in thinking about Go: the question it seeks to answer is whether or not a given move will more likely make it win the game. As we discussed, the winning state of Go is straightforward: if no more stones can be placed or are placed by players, the player whose stones occupy or surround most of the game board's area wins. By some meaningful contrast, we really don't know the "winning condition" of literature (otherwise, surely more books would be great). In his vociferous jeremiad against the current trend toward institutional literary studies from McGurl onward, Christian Lorentzen says that an anonymous editor of his acquaintance "called her current method of acquiring books 'throwing shit at the wall' to see what sticks" (2024). We are all very familiar with the stories of *Harry Potter*'s rejection by a dozen publishers and low initial print run, or

Lolita's being published by a French softcore porn publisher after being rejected by Nabokov's usual press.[21] A brief glance at the list of Pulitzer, Nobel, or even Booker Prize winners since these prizes' inception indicates how fleeting recognition in the spaces of consecration (Leypoldt 2016) is. If publishers and institutions don't reliably pick up either bestsellers or future mainstays in the literary canon, neither do they reliably reject the worst, either for their financial bottom-line or in the judgment of readers, critics, or scholars.

It's evidently possible to overstress the entire notion laid out above, of networked creativity and superorganisms, their similarity to genAI and the general problem of understanding what it means to think literature absent the figure of the author. But it's also possible to underestimate its relevance for my discussion here. I am, as noted, far less interested in the horizon of potential genAI literature than in the limitations in the thinking about literary studies that genAI reveals. The simple point that we don't know what is possible through genAI isn't all that interesting. The assertion that genAI will not be able, structurally, technologically, by dint of its computation's limits or the data's, to produce what might intersubjectively be called "literature" by literary studies, is, at the very least, disputed, but also, frankly, meaningless. And that not just because what I (a literary scholar) and you (presumably at least literary scholarship-adjacent, highly educated, cultured, what have you) think "good" literature is, is also not what most people would think good literature is. For those people, genAI is already making literature indistinguishable as text from human writing. In the November 2024 study I already referenced, Brian Porter and Edouard Machery asked participants to identify poetry as either written by an AI or human. Randomly assigned one of ten canonical poets, the participants managed to correctly identify genAI poetry in 46.6% of cases—i.e., below the success rate expected for merely guessing. In a more recent, 2025 study, Chakrabarty, Ginsburg, and Dhillon went one step further, feeding both expert and lay readers lines which a generative transformer system produced after being trained on the writing of award-winning authors who had written in those authors' style. Here, not

[21] *Lolita*, of course, was not per se rejected for reasons of its literary quality, even were it possible to abstract such a quality: it was rejected because publishing it would have been (as it was) a moral scandal. But insofar as its current status as a "literary" text is, at least also, a counterclaim to its scandalousness, this point does not detract from the one I'm trying to make here: we don't "know" what "good" literature is.

only were readers statistically unable to differentiate between genAI and human written texts—they in fact preferred the genAI versions to the actual human writing. In light of this, let me try out a proposition. All considerations of quality in literature *or* literary studies run afoul of genAI, if not yet in current practice, then in future possibility. And because versions of quality, "good" poetry, "causal" narratives, and so on, are all we have to disqualify genAI literary production on right now, we are in a bind. As a means of bounding off genAI literature from human-written literature, quality thus is the apparently best, but still an implausible category. And that appears true about all of the other ad hoc categories delimiting genAI creation from human creation. In various ways, if they're not circular, they're begging the question: they all insist that computers won't be able to write literature because they're not humans, because only humans can write literature.

Chiang, in one of the more obvious gambits of his essay, notes that AlphaZero—the general-purpose successor to the Go-winning AI that features in Labatut's *The MANIAC*—required 44 million games that it played against itself in order to become winning at chess. By contrast, a group of rats trained in driving little cars to a food source only required 23 tries to become secure at driving, a task that, as observing the behavior of "autonomous" cars has shown, is really not that easy. In explicating what he thinks this means, Chiang picks up a distinction that the Google researcher François Chollet has made (2019): that there's a necessary distinction between "skill" and "intelligence." "Skill," for Chollet, is how well you do a thing; "intelligence" is how well you gain skills. The latter, of course, is traditionally what AI research has been striving for. But "skill" is all you're basically getting. When AlphaZero plays 44 million games to get best at chess, it emerges as a skilled (very, very skilled) opponent, but not as a very intelligent one—less intelligent, perhaps, than the car-driving rats. Again, though: that's not the key issue. As I noted above, I'm fully aware of the fact that genAI is a misnomer: there's probably nothing meaningfully "intelligent" about what genAI does, though the measure of "intelligence" itself is a troubling ethical problem (see, for instance and popularly, Gould 1996). The point I've been making all along is that the measure of literary quality we're used to employing is not the level of intelligence, effort, knowledge, heartfeltness, and so on put into a text: it's what the text, when read, appears to show. In other words: any sufficiently skillful text would—by definition—look like intelligence, simply because you, as the reader, will never know the difference.

It is no doubt the case that, if we arrive at genAI literary production that is indistinguishable from human literary production, that genAI literary production will have been sourced from human literary production. It may even have been trained on human value assessments—including supervised learning, i.e., "curation"; indeed, it will almost inevitably have been propelled through some of the same channels of curation that current human literary production goes through. But to say that this genAI would never have learned to write like Shakespeare without being fed Shakespeare just is not very helpful when you're faced with the problem of *having* genAI Shakespeare, or if not Shakespeare, then at least A.I. Byatt. It may be true, but it'll be immaterial for the problem we're discussing here.

The moment genAI sets the fault lines of contemporary literary studies in stark relief: it exposes the ways in which we sit uneasily between positions about the very idea of "literature" and the ways we can possibly engage with it—indeed, what we hold to be true about this very object of the discipline. GenAI does not fundamentally challenge these takes on literature so much as expose them for a thin veneer overlaying a haphazardly constructed edifice: it requires us to come to terms with the haphazardness, the incommensurability of our different takes on literature (from Shakespeare's genius to networked creativity).

In so doing, it does more: it asks us to reconsider the role and position of literary studies from the ground up. In the next chapter, this will be the central issue: what the challenge of genAI means practically—at least imaginably—for the discipline. This question is prompted, yes, by the challenge to the idea of the literary that genAI poses. But it is also prompted by the challenge to our own textual production that genAI poses, whether speculatively or in real terms. GenAI is a moment, here as in the case of our thinking about literature, of reflexive opportunity: not just a bringer of anxieties, but also a horizon for our thinking about our narrow professional world. For literary studies, alas, the consequences of potential genAI literary production are formidable and potentially disruptive. Or, more precisely: they're *either* fundamental and disruptive, or they don't matter at all.

References

Altieri, Charles. 2024. Modes of Intelligence. In *The AI Revolution: Speculations on Authorship, Pedagogy, and the Future of the Profession*, edited by Nir Evron and Roi Tortakovsky. Special Issue of *Poetics Today* 45 (2): 207–214.

Bajohr, Hannes. 2023. Niemand schreibt allein (Nachwort zu *(Berlin, Miami)*). In *Berlin, Miami*, 239–267. Berlin: Matthes & Seitz.

Bajohr, Hannes. 2024. On Artificial and Post-artificial Texts: Machine Learning and the Reader's Expectations of Literary and Non-literary writing. In *The AI Revolution: Speculations on Authorship, Pedagogy, and the Future of the Profession*, edited by Nir Evron and Roi Tortakovsky. Special Issue of *Poetics Today* 45 (2): 331–361.

Baßler, Moritz. 2021. Der neue Midcult: Vom Wandel populärer Leserschaften als Herausforderung der Kritik. *Pop. Kultur und Kritik* 18:132–149.

Bender, Emily M., Timnit Gebru, Angelina McMillan-Major, and Shmargaret Shmitchell. 2021. On the Dangers of Stochastic Parrots: Can Language Models Be Too Big?. In *FAccT '21: Proceedings of the 2021 ACM Conference on Fairness, Accountability, and Transparency* (March), 610–623.

Bertram, Lillian-Yvonne, and Nick Montfort. 2024. *Output: An Anthology of Computer-Generated Text, 1953–2023*. Cambridge and London: MIT Press and Denver and New York: Counterpath.

Bosse, Heinrich. 2014. *Autorschaft ist Werkherrschaft: Über die Entstehung des Urheberrechts aus dem Geist der Goethezeit*. Paderborn: Fink.

Bourdieu, Pierre. 1996. *The Rules of Art: Genesis and Structure of the Literary Field*. Cambridge: Polity Press.

Breithaupt, Fritz. 2023. *The Narrative Brain: The Stories Our Neurons Tell*. New Haven: Yale University Press.

Brouillette, Sarah. 2024. The Author as Social Production. (Review). *Studies in the Novel* 56 (1): 99–1045.

Burrow, Colin. 2019. *Imitating Authors: From Plato to Futurity*. Oxford: Oxford University Press.

Chakrabarty, Tuhin, Jane C. Ginsburg, and Paramveer Dhillon. 2025. Readers Prefer Outputs of AI Trained on Copyrighted Books over Expert Human Writers. *Columbia Law Research Paper* 5605670. Online.

Chiang, Ted. 2024. Why A.I. Isn't Going to Make Art. *The New Yorker*, August 31. Online.

Childress, Clayton. 2017. *Under the Cover: The Creation, Production, and Reception of a Novel*. Princeton: Princeton University Press.

Clune, Michael. 2019. *A Defense of Judgment*. Chicago: University of Chicago Press.

Comitta, Tom. 2025. *People's Choice Literature: The Most Wanted & Unwanted Novels*. New York: Columbia University Press.

Davis, Joshua, et al. 2024. The Temperature Feature of ChatGPT: Modifying Creativity for Clinical Research. *JMIR Human Factors*, March 8.

DeCosmo, Leonardo. 2022. Google Engineer Claims AI Chatbot Is Sentient: Why That Matters. *Scientific American*, July 12. Online.

Dreyfus, Hubert L., and Stuart E. Dreyfus. 1988. Making a Mind versus Modelling the Brain: Artificial Intelligence Back at a Branchpoint. *Daedalus* 117 (1): 15–43.

Dziri, Nouha, et al. 2022. On the Origin of Hallucinations in Conversational Models: Is it the Datasets or the Models? In *Proceedings of the 2022 Conference of the North American Chapter of the Association for Computational Linguistics: Human Language Technologies*, 5271–5285.

Eaglestone, Robert. 2019. *Literature: Why It Matters*. London: Polity.

Eagleton, Terry. 2008. *Literary Theory: An Introduction*. Minneapolis: University of Minnesota Press.

Elam, Michelle. 2023. Poetry Will Not Optimize; or, What is Literature to AI. *American Literature* 95 (2): 281–303.

Feige, Daniel Martin. 2025. *Kritik der Digitalisierung: Technik, Rationalität und Kunst*. Hamburg: Meiner.

Fletcher, Angus. 2021. Why Computers Will Never Read (or Write) Literature. *Narrative* 29 (1): 1–28.

Fletcher, Angus. 2022. Why Computer AI Will Never Do What We Imagine It Can. *Narrative* 30 (1): 114–137.

Fletcher, Angus. 2024. Shakespeare Didn't Brainstorm: Why Literature Proves That There's More to Intelligence than AI. In *The Routledge Handbook of AI and Literature*, edited by Will Slocombe and Genevieve Lively, 125–135. London: Routledge.

Franklin, Samuel. 2023. *The Cult of Creativity: A Surprisingly Recent History*. Chicago: University of Chicago Press.

Gould, Stephen Jay. 1996. *The Mismeasure of Man*. New York: Norton.

Grankowski, Alex, Stephen M. Downes, and Partick Forber. 2024. LLMS are Not Just Next Token Predictors. *arXiv.org*. Online.

Guillory, John. 2024. *On Close Reading*. Chicago and London: University of Chicago Press.

Harris, Mark. 2012. TV's Best Talker: Aaron Sorkin on The Newsroom, Sorkinism, and Sounding Smart. *Vulture*. Online.

Hayles, N. Katherine. 2022. Inside the Mind of an AI: Materiality and the Crisis of Representation. *New Literary History* 53 (4)/54 (1): 635–666.

Henricksen, Leah. 2024. Conversations with No One. In *The AI Revolution: Speculations on Authorship, Pedagogy, and the Future of the Profession*, edited by Nir Evron and Roi Tortakovsky. Special Issue of *Poetics Today* 45 (2): 291–299.

Kirschenbaum, Matthew, and Rita Raley. 2024. AI and the University as a Service. *PMLA* XXX:1–12.

Knapp, Steven, and Walter Benn Michaels. 1982. Against Theory. *Critical Inquiry* 8 (4): 723–742.

Knapp, Steven, and Walter Benn Michaels. 2023. Here is a Wave Poem that I Wrote…I Hope You Like It! In *Again Theory: A Forum on Language, Meaning, and Intent in a Time of Stochastic Parrots*, edited by Matthew Kirschenbaum. *Critical Inquiry*, Online.

Kraus, Kari. 2023. A View from the Periscope. In *Again Theory: A Forum on Language, Meaning, and Intent in a Time of Stochastic Parrots.* edited by Matthew Kirschenbaum. *Critical Inquiry*, Online.

Lanzendörfer, Tim. 2025. You Can't Say That: The Serious Limits of Literary Studies Creativity. *Creativecritical.net.* Online.

Lanzendörfer, Tim. forthcoming. Facetious Criticism; Or: Why We Don't Have to Mean What We Say.

Lewinsky, Charles. 2024. *Täuschend Echt.* Zürich: Diogenes.

Leypoldt, Günter. 2016. Degrees of Public Relevance: Walter Scott and Toni Morrison. *Modern Language Quarterly* 77 (2): 369–393.

Leypoldt, Günter. 2025. *Literature's Social Lives: A Socio-Institutional History of Literary Value.* Oxford: Oxford University Press.

Lindsey, Jack, et al. 2025. On the Biology of a Large Language Model. *Transformer Circuits.* Online.

Lorentzen, Christian. 2024. Literature Without Literature. *Granta* 168. Online.

Macherey, Pierre. 1978. *A Theory of Literary Production.* London: Routledge.

Marcinkowski, Michael. 2024. There Has Never Been an Intelligent Literature. In *The Routledge Handbook of AI and Literature*, edited by Will Slocombe and Genevieve Lively, 113–124. London: Routledge.

McGurl, Mark. 2009. *The Program Era: Postwar Fiction and the Rise of Creative Writing.* Cambridge: Harvard University Press.

Moretti, Franco. 1998. *Atlas of the European Novel 1800–1900.* London: Verso.

Moss, Adam. 2024. *The Work of Art: How Something Comes from Nothing.* New York: Penguin.

Ottman, Klaus. 1986. Jeff Koons 1986 Interview. Quoted from https://libbys-niche.blogspot.com/2009/08/jeffkoons-1986-interview.html; originally in *Journal of Contemporary Art*, October 1986.

Pasquinelli, Matteo. 2023. *The Eye of the Master. A Social History of Artificial Intelligence.* London: Verso.

Perlow, Seth. 2024. Generative Theories, Pretrained Responses: Large AI Models and the Humanities. *PMLA* 139 (3): 548–522.

Porter, Brian, and Edouard Machery. 2024. AI-Generated Poetry is Indistinguishable from Human-Written Poetry and Is Rated More Favorably. *Nature: Scientific Reports* 14. Online.

Rettberg, Scott. 2019. *Electronic Literature.* Cambridge: Wiley.

Roach, Rebecca. 2025. *Programming Literature*. Oxford: Oxford University Press.
Santana-Acuña, Alváro. 2020. *Ascent to Glory: How One Hundred Years of Solitude Was Written and Became a Global Classic*. New York: Columbia University Press.
Sawyer, Keith N., and Danah Henriksen. 2024. *Explaining Creativity: The Science of Human Innovation*. Oxford: Oxford University Press.
Sinykin, Dan. 2023. *Big Fiction: How Conglomeration Changed the Publishing Industry and American Literature*. New York: Columbia University Press.
Thorne, Sarah. 2019. Hey Siri, Tell Me a Story: Digital Storytelling and AI Authorship. *Convergence: The International Journal of Research into New Media Technologies* 26 (4): 808–823.
Turing, Alan M. 1950. Computing Machinery and Intelligence. *Mind* 59 (236): 433–460.
Williams, Raymond. 1977. *Marxism and Literature*. Oxford: Oxford University Press.
Winterson, Jeanette. 2025. OpenAI's Metafictional Short Story About Grief is Beautiful and Moving. *The Guardian*, March 12.
Wooldridge, Michael. 2020. *A Brief History of Artificial Intelligence: What it Is, Where We Are, and Where We Are Going*. New York: Flatiron Books.

CHAPTER 3

Post-AI Literary Studies

Abstract This chapter expands from the discussions around the nature of literature as the object of literary studies to the questions which genAI raises specifically for literary studies. It suggests that even though the changes which genAI has made, makes, or will make to the object of literary studies, i.e., literature itself, are disciplinarily potentially less fundamental than those made to disciplinary practices themselves. It begins from the observation that our epistemology rests on notions of plausibility and text-to-text relation that immediately relate us to genAI text-making practices. It argues this point in relation to genAI's performance in other disciplines and points out that recent attempts to describe literary studies as creative, as craft, and as skilled practice all appear to reiterate the reflexive humanism of our understanding of literature, but, in an age of genAI, suddenly appear fraught. It suggests that existing discussions of literary studies' relationship to genAI underestimate this problem, because they focus on our object rather than disciplinary practices themselves. Ultimately, the chapter suggests, what emerges from attention to genAI potentialities is a devaluing of our outputs as expressions of literary studies work.

Keywords Literary studies • Literary theory • Creativity • Literary sociology • Artificial intelligence • Literature • Craft • Skill • Literary quality • Authorship

T. Lanzendörfer, *AI and the Challenge to Literary Studies*,
https://doi.org/10.1007/978-3-032-25526-6_3

What a cop out! But bear with me.

Whatever we thought literature, the object of literary studies, was a couple of years back: at least we could be sure it wasn't made by genAI. But even today, depending on what we think "literature" encompasses, we can't, really. Our characters might have been given backstories by ChatGPT, or their facial features might have been suggested by Dall-E. The short story we're reading might no longer be helpfully flagged by the *Guardian* before printing; or we're caught up in an experiment in which a computer scientist wants to find out if we can distinguish the writing of a Nobel laureate from a genAI system trained on that laureate's writing. Would we be willing to bet we notice genAI's voice now? (Clearly, we shouldn't.) In the future, it's possible we may be even less certain what in a novel, or indeed what novel, has been written by humans, and what by genAI. *Literature*, I have just now suggested, understood in the way we tend to understand it, is a category which genAI requires us to question, specifically because it seems plausible for genAI to become capable of reproducing anything *textual* about the kinds of texts we discuss as literature. It reveals to us, as a discipline, the aporias of our thinking about literature, our ostensible object. With apologies to Slavoj Žižek, it looks like we clearly know that, in our activities, we are following an illusion, but we're still doing it (see 2008, 30). But more than that, genAI should also make us question ourselves, and our textual production as literary scholars, seeing as how we are, very much, nothing but producers of plausible texts. This has consequences, consequences we're already witnessing. As a discipline, we are now in what Pierre-Héli Monot has called a moment of "robopathy": a "retrospective questioning of self-attributed markers of individuation, caused by processes of technological innovation" (2023, 84, my own translation). At least we *should* be—this will be the major argument of the following pages. And the major reason we should be is because we, ourselves, as literary scholars, are merely producers of texts, wordsmiths with a specific shared object, devices for producing sentences in response to sentences, to adopt a line from the philosopher Hilary Putnam (1981, 10).

My point in the preceding section has not been, to reiterate, to make a very specific and definite claim about the nature of future genAI literary production. Rather, it has been to suggest that notwithstanding all our philosophical, theoretical, and literary sociological work decentering the creative author in the production of fiction, we nonetheless habitually return to her as a figure authorizing, literally, our engagement with literature. I've argued in the previous chapter that genAI literary production sets into sharp relief assumptions about the object of literary studies that, in light of genAI, become both harder to defend and perhaps, in the last instance, less necessary to defend.

But at the same time, this discussion of genAI literature merely prepares the ground for what follows below, a discussion what genAI means for the practice of literary studies more widely understood. The uncertain, shaky grounds of our object simply point us to the unstable foundations of all of our own work. Thinking about the category of "literature" is at best ancillary to the problems of post-genAI literary studies, insofar as literary studies is already hardly bound by a specifically "literary" object in practice, by conventional literariness. Against this background, the challenge which genAI produces for literary studies also needs to be split. As far as genAI as a producer of our textual *objects* is concerned, it may well be possible to ignore or integrate it in various ways. As far as genAI as a producer of our textual *outputs* is concerned, we should be clear about its potential actual and necessary theoretical impact.

What is involved in the discussions we're having around the future of literary studies under post-genAI conditions tend to be the concepts informing our job, rather than the very fundamentals of the job. We see in genAI questions about what literature means, what interpretation could be, what comprehension is, what an author is, or what would be entailed in considering genAI an author, and so on, rather than what it might mean that knowing these things, or better, producing texts about these things does not signify our exclusionary professional expertise anymore. Some of these discussions we are having, as we will see, in fact echo what we've already heard about creativity, craft, human ingenuity, and the role which institutions play in the concrete way in which we produce texts. The problems facing genAI *me* are fundamentally the same as those facing A.I. Byatt: chiefly, producing textual forms that cohere plausibly, often over hundreds of pages, indeed offer a form of narrative reasoning; but also shorter arguments that either are, or give the illusion of being, research papers and conference presentations and reviews, and the like.[1] All of these texts are

[1] At the same time, the problems I have may exceed the problems which A.S. Byatt has, because the scholarly bent of literary studies evacuates the key problem of authorial authority and intention even more thoroughly. Double-blind peer review allegorizes the idea that we, as human beings, do not matter for the usefulness of our outputs; what matters is the internal plausibility of these outputs. That is less true for literary production in practice, where public audiences, at least, are invested in authorial authenticity.

plausible, useful, and valid outputs only to the extent that they are so as texts—and as texts only.

The central suggestion in this section will be that I, you, and the colleagues you share the departmental hallways with are at least as much (but also as little) in danger of being replaced by genAI as A.S. Byatt is by A.I. Byatt. Whether we are replaceable in fact or not turns partially—as it did in the previous chapter—on the capacities we are willing to attribute to genAI, and here as there, we'll just assume the best-worst: the case in which genAI produces text that is indistinguishable from human writing. Whether we are replaceable or not in this case boils down to the question of what we understand our actual work to be, and what we should understand our work to be comes into clearer perspective through the question of *what* about what we understand our work to be would be replaceable by the best version of genAI. And to be frank, it is not likely that it matters what we understand our work to be—it will be for others to decide the ultimate fate of our departments. It's quite difficult for me to follow Seth Perlow's argument that "humanities scholars, especially those studying interpretive theories and methodologies, are uniquely equipped to address the challenges that large AI models pose." But, given the way in which our self-understanding is bound up in how we might make others value our work, this appears only logical as a claim: keep us around, we get this stuff. But there's more to it than that. Perlow suggests that "we embrace literature for its resistance to rigid logic, its nuance and ambiguity, and modern criticism offers a robust tool kit for rigorous thinking at the limits of knowledge" (2024, 550). Perlow here goes beyond an instrumental claim, and names the default disciplinary position on our social role. I would hesitate to say that it has been shown to be true that we have such a "robust tool kit."[2] But in the final analysis, I am arguing almost the

[2] It's only very slightly unfair, perhaps, to point here to the opening of Nan Z. Da's essay on literary criticism and AI (2025), where Da cites "an excellent literary critic" on the famous Emily Dickinson poem "Because I could not stop for Death." Da quotes him as follows: "'Think about it,' he said. 'You have to be ahead of Death—ahead in a race, ahead in a timed task—to stop for it or not stop for it. At the same time Death has to be ahead of you to stop for you or not stop for you'" (103). I read this at a bus stop, where, kindly, my bus stopped for me. I was "ahead" of it on its route, I guess, but hardly in a race with it or engaged in a timed task with it; and even though the bus was behind me, *it* stopped for *me*. Or, more simply put: the excellent literary critic is simply wrong, wrong at a simple task of adjudicating what a line in a poem must imply; and *New Left Review*'s presumably robust reviewing process did not catch the issue. If this example is anecdotal, it's also telling.

opposite when I suggest that humanities scholars are particularly endangered by the challenges of large-language genAI models, precisely because our tool kits may not be all that robust in an age when it has been opened wholesale to use by those very genAI models.

There are two dimensions, I think, to the question of "post-artificial" literary studies: the first, already partially broached above, concerns the hermeneutic situation, the question of the "possible consequences of large language models and related technologies for interpretive situations and hermeneutic strategies" (Bajohr 2024, 333). The majority of scholarship and thought concerning genAI's impact on the discipline of literary studies has been foregrounding this question, if implicitly in discussions around the status of genAI "literary" writing (for instance, Catani 2023; Slocombe and Lively 2024). The second, by some contrast, has been underthought: it is the question of what concrete impact genAI textual production has on the production of literary studies knowledge—on our own outputs. And, by extension, what this thinking about our outputs means for the discipline of literary studies and its understanding of its own role in, well, the world at large. I want to pursue this question most extensively in what follows.

My focus in terms of literary studies is interpretation. It bears acknowledging that not all literary studies work is interpretation—some of it is archival, some of it is editorial, some of it is, increasingly, sociological (as we saw above). At the same time, interpretation sits at the core of our curricula and our disciplinary identity as literary studies professionals. And it's crucial to me to highlight here the need to understand the problem as being about far more than just our relation to digital literature or specifically to interpretative problems thrown up by genAI, among which is the problem of literary scholars interpreting genAI text. Here, the question is, as Eric Hayot puts it, not "whether such work can be interpreted. Of course it can. Anything can be interpreted if you want to interpret it. I mean, how are we supposed to interpret it? What kind of evidence is it? What can you use it to prove or understand?" (2014, 280).[3] Hayot departs from the assumption that there are "intention levels" that authorize interpretative engagement with a text. And for him, the ultimate question is: "Can LLM-produced language function as humanist evidence, and if so, how?" (281). Yes, as Hannes Bajohr points out, given both the acknowl-

[3] As we go a little deeper into the question of intention below, it'll become apparent that Hayot's insistent "of course" is not universally shared.

edged current and potential future capacities of genAI, and even more so, the ubiquitousness of its outputs, "practitioners of the hermeneutic disciplines [...] are called to consider what impact the current rapid advances in machine learning research might have on the way in which we understand and interpret text" (2024, 332). Yes, as both N. Katherine Hayles and Matthew Kirschenbaum suggest, it's true that "new interpretive strategies are necessary for machine-generated narratives" (Hayles 2024, 646).[4]

This, though, is essentially a language-world issue, not a language-literary studies issue, i.e.: it's about whether something a genAI textually outputs can be interpreted in the same way (as giving evidence of meaning in the world) as literature by humans; it's not about whether or not it could serve as literary studies evidence about textual meaning. In other words, the point Hayot, Bajohr, and Hayles all raise in different ways may for given answers suffice to disqualify genAI literature from consideration by literary scholars, but it doesn't disqualify genAI literary criticism because literary criticism does not have a text-world relation, only a text-text relation. As the German critic Erhard Schüttpelz recently pointed out, contemporary literary studies relies on the "lexical knowledge" of "sedimented" previous criticism (2023, 79, my translation), textually-mediated knowledge and judgments—as though we needed to be told. It is, in fact, a key part of our professionalism that we are not enjoined, but rather actively discouraged, from suggesting that our own experiential relation to the world matters to reading literature critically. We are enjoined, instead, to support our claims to the world-relevance of both our interpretations and the texts we study by *textual* citations.[5] It's about more than our understanding of text, it is about the work of the discipline as a whole. The problem we are faced with is less the question of what we do with genAI literary texts—it's, rather, what anyone would do with our interpretations when we can also have genAI interpretations. In a recent article in the *Chronicle of Higher Education*, Lee Konstantinou speaks for what one would assume is most of the discipline of literary studies: "the notion that one might automate the interpretation of literary texts [is] especially

[4] Without quibbling with the details of their argumentation, what is striking here is that the fundamental assumption of these writers appears to be that because texts exist, therefore they are in need of interpretation. Given the way in which we disciplinarily already select our objects, that seems unnecessary as a conclusion, and I will briefly say something about that in the final section of this book.

[5] And just to be clear, I tend to theoretically support this stance as a matter of professional practice (see, inter alia, Lanzendörfer 2023).

galling" (2025). The question of automating interpretation is a question about meaning and interpretation, but it is also, if you'll forgive, about the meaning and value *of* interpretation: the question of what we're faced with when we're faced with our own computational reproducibility.

The thought that genAI might produce a sea change in a discipline is perhaps more thoroughly explored in the sciences than in the humanities (for what I suggest are somewhat puzzling reasons, given the humanities comparative inextricability from the medium genAI is especially good at working with, namely, text). It certainly bears pointing out that many of the systems which have been in the news regarding genAI advances in the sciences are not large-language models. The winners of the 2024 Nobel Prize in Chemistry, for instance, won for a generative AI, AlphaFold, which was specifically trained on science data, to solve science problems. This is where most of the hype about genAI comes from. Sam Altman, who's unlikely to be the winner of the Nobel Prize for Literature, unsurprisingly was straightforward in a 2024 article about the vision for the future of genAI in science. Among the things he believes AI will do are "fixing the climate, establishing a space colony, and the discovery of all of physics." There are considerable problems even with the idea that generative AI alone can do any of the things Altman hypes us up for, it should be said. AI, after all, cannot "discover" except in data provided to it, and for at least some of physics, it's precisely the data that's lacking. All the same, specifically-trained AIs, it appears clear, have a clear place in scientific research, and the hype notwithstanding, they do advance the boundaries of scientific inquiry.

It's important to situate these two versions of science uses of AI in the contemporary, the use of all potential versions of AI and the use of LLM genAI. The latter has, largely, shown itself to be a plaything for rich men who are altogether too full of themselves (but I repeat myself), men, and it is largely men, who think their success in one field or another means their intellectual acumen translates to any field they choose, and often does so in what has come to be called "vibe science." When these men turn to genAI to discuss their fancy ideas for physics or medicine breakthroughs, their chatbot sparing partners tend to confirm the correctness of their assumptions with plausible, but empirically false, extrapolations of their thought (see, for instance, Alberto et al. 2025). At the same time, the more generalized generative AI of large-language models has also seen success for some time now. In 2023, for instance, a large-language model solved a hitherto unsolved math problem (Heaven 2023). In mid-2025, researchers at Google's DeepMind and OpenAI announced that their LLMs were performing maths at Mathematics Olympiad winning levels (Castelvecchi 2025; cf. Zeraoulia 2025). But, as Paul Schmidt and Amnon Meir have pointed out (2023), mostly generative LLM AI will be a mixed blessing in scientific writing at best.[6]

As Steven Knapp and Walter Benn Michaels point out, there is no really obvious path from AI's analysis of biomolecular systems to, well, anything really: no matter how complex the systems, and they may very well be much more complex than human language (though perhaps not), they do not tend to raise interpretative problems. Instead, they end up producing descriptions of cause-and-effect relationships that "always seem to mean what they say, ... because they don't mean anything at all" (2023). In other words: the simple idea of transitioning from the experiences in the sciences to the experience of the literary humanities is a problem, in that our work is a categorically different one. I do not disagree. However, I think we miss the point of both the potential horizon of genAI and the problem of meaning when we, as Knapp and Michaels appear to do, simply exclude the potential of genAI to make plausible assertions of meaning about text. Large-language model genAI is not generally reliable at science for a fairly simple reason. The results of scientific inquiry are not bound to plausibility for their validity, but to text-external truth—at the very least, something like an actual solution. Simply put, it's wildly insufficient to suggest that a particular protein plausibly *could* be folded like this, when in fact, it *cannot* be folded like this. Specifically trained AI systems often do well with such empirical questions, whereas LLMs generally do not. LLMs are specifically trained systems, too, though: on language use.[7]

It is unlikely that we will see a genAI that is specifically trained on literary criticism and only the kinds of books that literary criticism generally works on, of course, and this may hinder its ability to do our work in the near future, anyway. But at the same time, as I have been at pains to point out: that's not the point so much as it is an easy way out of the theoretical

[6] And similarly, recent research has also suggested that LLMs do not really code well; see Kwa et al. (2025).

[7] We might also hear echoes here of Foucault's differentiation between founders of discourses and founders of sciences. Questions of validity in expanding the discourse, Foucault points out, recur to reworking, reappraising, and reinterpreting the foundational work (i.e., a text); in sciences, the question of validity will always be (for instance) "what physics or cosmology *is*" (1998/1969, 219).

problem. Let me frame it like this: the fundamental theoretical issue which genAI faces us with is that if literary criticism is a thing that can be "learned" by "knowing" all existing literary criticism, and iterating repeatedly on it, genAI can learn it. (Conversely, if we think it can't be learned by knowing all previous literary criticism and iterating on it, how do we think it can be learned?). As of this moment, we can be pretty sure that the first condition of this hypothetical, genAI's inclusive knowledge of previous literary criticism, is simply a fact. We should assume that everything you and I have ever published is already part of the training data of current LLMs. As *The Atlantic* revealed, Meta's Llama 3 model at least was, in full awareness of the liminal legality of the move, trained on data from the pirate website Library Genesis, which includes a vast amount of academic publications among its 7.5 million books and 81 million research papers (Reisner 2025), aside from publically-available pre-print databases such as Pubmed or ArXiv. My books, for what it is worth, are also on there.[8] The second condition of this hypothetical, that literary criticism is as a process of learning, a version of iterating on the existent, is perhaps a bit more fraught. I will address it in more detail below with reference to recent work in the sociology of literary studies, attempts at actually tracing the practice of literary studies work, which—at the very least—does not really bear out the notion that it is anything else than iteration.

Some recent scholarship has already hinted that the possibility that the discipline's work as such is under threat by genAI, though, as I will try to suggest, it does not go far enough. Most exhaustively, Nir Evron has suggested that in the contemporary moment, any "form of textual production that relies on repeated formal patterns and generic conventions—which is to say, most forms of textual production—is vulnerable, if not by the technology in its current state, then by its near-future iterations" (2024, 317). Perhaps the easiest target is what he dubs the "rote academic article," an object we all know, but few of us criticize enough: "the kind of research that applies a familiar set of theoretical maneuvers to a text in order to find its own theoretical assumptions confirmed." This, Evron avers, "is now mechanically reproducible and hence obsolete" (2024, 322).[9] As I've insisted several times

[8] According to *The Atlantic*, OpenAI has denied using Library Genesis in training its models.

[9] One possible counterpoint to all this doom-and-glooming is that the content of literary criticism's textual work cannot be reduced to its syntagmatic plausibility, that is to say: that we shouldn't confuse the idea of the plausible sentence (i.e., this is a sentence one could plausibly write) with the idea of the plausible claim about a text (i.e., this is a sentence one

now, I think we can actually forego both the diagnosis of current reproducibility and the prognosis of an inevitable future and suggest that genAI's theoretical horizon also does this work of rendering us vulnerable.

At the heart of Evron's discussion of the matter lies, as it were, an epistemological question: what kind of knowledge-work does our current literary studies formation undertake? What, and how, does literary studies know? To Evron, and I am heavily sympathetic here, much of our current work cannot be said to produce anything new. At the same time, some of our work, Evron insists, can: there still is "creative, historically sensitive, and politically conscious" work that is in the "best tradition of our profession" (318).

What does such work—whether rote or in the best tradition of the profession—actually do, though? As Jeffrey Binder has recently noted, "a striking aspect" of many of the claims about genAI cheerleading is how "it locates knowledge in language" (2022, 2). The epistemological problems thrown up by genAI are especially relevant to literary studies because of this overlap with a general truth about genAI: our reliance on textual evidence, absent outside referents that could reliably adjudicate truth claims, and our reliance on textual production in order to communicate these plausible truth claims. We draw many of the same lines between good and terrible literature that we draw between good academic writing and bad: good academic writing is creative and original, for instance. Certainly, we may also tentatively assign other categories to good academic writing, such as "truth" or "reliability," and potentially even so strong a category as "knowledge" as something which is produced by literary studies. But importantly, all of these categories remain textual in nature; and in so far as genAI is potentially at least a skilled producer of text, the absence of categorical differences between genAI and human literary studies knowledge production obtrudes heavily. As Binder puts it, genAI is "implicitly aligned with [a] social sort of meaning: whatever significance [say] the word 'sum' may have in its outputs stems from how that word has been used by people" (223). As Ted Chiang summarizes the question: "if a large language model has compiled a vast number of correlations between economic terms–so many that it can offer plausible responses to a wide

could plausibly write *about this text*). This complaint echoes Nan Z. Da's point about the difficulty of literature (as a specific kind of text), which, to her, "cannot be expressed as the sum of semantic difficulty and grammatical difficulty" (2025, 123). This confusion of registers, I hope, will be cleared up below.

variety of questions–should we say that it actually understands economic theory?" As I might go on to ask: If a large language model has compiled a vast number of correlations between things to say about *Moby Dick* and Marxism–so many that it can offer plausible responses to a wide variety of questions–should we say that it actually understands Marxist criticism of *Moby Dick*?

Put like that, the question is wrong, of course, simply in focusing on the issue of "understanding"—as we already saw in the section on genAI literature. The Turing test already suggested in the 1950s that it is not useful to say "the computer thinks like a human," because the consequences of the computer thinking, and the computer emulating thinking responses, is not just the same: it literally makes no sense to quibble about the words used to describe the route taken to get to these responses. Whether the computer "thinks" its way to being "like" a human, or "just" computes its way there—who can tell? N. Katherine Hayles, in this sense, is just like the Google engineer who thought his chatbot was conscious when she suggests that we need to understand GPT-4's output of reasoning-like text as manifesting reasoning—reasoning "evidenced in its pervasive use of because in its responses" (2024, 261). Saying "because" no more evidences reasoning than saying "I love you" evidences emotions—or, for that matter, that because computers cannot "think" narratively, they cannot produce text that makes narrative-causal sense.

Similarly, the question of whether genAI "understands" "Marxist criticism" is moot. I think that, in my rewriting of Chiang's example, it really doesn't matter if genAI *understands* anything about *Moby Dick* or Marxism. The relevant question is this: if that computer model has compiled a vast number of Marxist literary studies concepts, so many that it can offer a plausible Marxist reading of *Moby Dick*, has it written Marxist criticism on *Moby Dick*? And has it produced knowledge? That's a far harder question to answer, though some have tried. N. Katherine Hayles, for instance, suggests that the GPT-3 model already "may be understood as expressing a kind of intuitive or tacit knowledge that it has gained from countless indexical correlations." For Hayles, this is "what makes its texts suitable objects for literary studies" (2024, 650). In Hayles's discussion, the question is more about the relation between literature and world, again, and the commonsense notion that unless literature expresses something like "knowledge" about the world, it's possibly not worth attending to. For me here, this raises the question what, if anything, makes out the specialness of literary criticism—whether it does not make GPT-3 or its successors a suitable *subject* in literary criticism. As Chiang asks: "is it possible that statistical regularities in text actually do correspond to genuine knowledge of the real world" (2024)? Can statistical regularities correspond to knowledge about *Moby Dick*? We might also ask if we think that the plausible texts we write about *Moby Dick* correspond to—or, indeed are—such knowledge; and if so, of what order that knowledge is, and what it signifies about our relation to genAI textual production.

In some ways, this is just a reframing of a fairly old question in literary studies. Its "lack of intention," writes Chiang, "is why ChatGTP is not actually using language." If it's not "using language," if it's not intentional, if it's merely stochastic, it's not worth attending to—anymore, say, than the not-quite writing created by the waves on the beach in Steven Knapp and Walter Benn Michael's "Against Theory" (1982). In that famous essay, Knapp and Michaels imagine a situation in which, beach-walking, you encounter, written in the sand, the first stanza of Wordsworth's "A Slumber Did My Spirit Seal." As you gaze upon the text, Knapp and Michaels aver, you may think about the text's intentionality absent an author—simply because the default assumption would be that so complex a text is authored. But then a second wave washes the stanza away and replaces it with the second stanza of the same poem. Now, Knapp and Michaels say, you're faced with two possibilities: either you assume intention in the wave (the living sea, or the ghost of Wordsworth) or you do not—but in the latter case, you must acknowledge that they are simply word-like erosions of the sand, mere marks. In point of fact, this is a confusing way of putting things. What Knapp and Michaels are after is not the status of the words/not-words on the beach (whether or not they "are" words): rather, they are after the position you must take toward them in order for them to be words. To say they are words, they suggest, is to insist they are intentional, even if the agent of their intentionality is a ghost, a sea god, or a computer. To Knapp and Michaels, as Lisa Siraganian has summarized, the whole point of the argument is that "the preliminary step for interpreting *is* the presumption of intention" (2023).

Several contributors to a 2023 *Critical Inquiry* in the Moment exchange (among others) have pointed out that genAI seems to complicate this situation. Seth Perlow, for instance, replying directly to Knapp and Michaels's "Against Theory," straightforwardly announces: "the marks will remain legible."[10] Hannes Bajohr speaks of the "ambiguous object that is artificial text" (2023) that forces us to "*suspend* the question of intention and read it as meaningful nevertheless." Similarly, Alex Gil suggests: "Going forward, most of us will only have time to look for useful meaning, not intention, for better or worse" (2023), as a consequence of genAI text production. For these critics, the specific way in which genAI produces text is a fundamental departure from the simple duality intentional/non-intentional that Knapp and Michaels adopted, and the underlying assumption is that there will be no way to identify the difference between genAI writing and human writing anymore.[11]

In fact, of course, many of the arguments made here in response to the challenge of genAI track very well on earlier criticisms of "Against Theory" or the intentionalist school's earlier work to which Knapp and Michaels responded—such as the very apropos line in Peter Juhl's *Interpretation* which suggested that if the Wordsworth poem had been "accidentally typed out by a monkey depressing keys on a typewriter" (1981, 71), then we need to consider an (actual) "agent's (the author's) motive, reason, purpose, or intentions" (74). GenAI, I agree with Knapp and Michaels, does nothing radical at all to the question of intention and meaning. As

[10] In doing so, Perlow tracks Toril Moi's discussion of the episode in *Revolution of the Ordinary*, where she insists that you cannot acknowledge the words on the beach as marks after you've recognized them as words. As she asks: "How am I expected to achieve this?" Knapp and Michaels's point, however, is precisely that you've misrecognized them as words (2023), because we tend to assume intentionality for such utterances. And you needn't force yourself to the conclusion that they are words: you just must acknowledge that if you still insist they are words, which is just to say that you read them as having meaning, then you have signally expanded the realm of intentional agents.

[11] The differentiation between intention/meaning and non-intention/non-meaning may appear to track onto the distinction I rejected above, between a short story and the illusion of a short story. In that distinction, you may *think* you are reading a short story, but in fact, you are just reading—to adopt Knapp and Michaels's terms—marks that look like a short story. This is not an implausible reading, but I think the cases are different. The distinction between the short story and the illusion of the short story is not, I think, intention as Knapp and Michaels address it; they explicitly reject the distinction that is operative in the case Fletcher presented, namely that between textual and authorial intention. Fletcher suggests that because there is no actual authorial (agential, determinative, pre-textual) intention in the illusion of a short story, therefore ascription of intention is not possible. Knapp and Michaels point out that ascription of intention is always ascription of authorial intention after the fact. In reading the short story as a short story, you have ascribed it the status of an intentional object; if you refuse to read it because you don't think genAI can make literature, you also have made a decision about what kinds of agents in the world count as intentional agents.

Lisa Siraganian puts it in her contribution to the exchange: "The conjecture of intention is required to make the signifier meaningful as a sign—whether that intention is correctly identified or totally misinterpreted, whether it remains uncertain or is, after the fact, denied by readers" (2023).

My point in reiterating this discussion is not to open another front in the question of genAI literature. It merely lays important groundwork for the problem that is key to me: how we envisage literary studies work to be produced—in particular, when a reading of *Moby Dick* is in fact a reading of *Moby Dick*. My contention here is that the system by which we decide these things is pretty much the same as the one that is operative in the discussion of literary meaning. If the waves striking the beach produced, instead of the first and then second stanzas of Wordsworth's poem, the first and then second paragraphs of a reading of *Moby Dick*, we would be facing the same issue, but for literary studies: if we accepted the reading as a reading, we would have accepted the wave as an intentional agent.

It's too facile to say that there's nothing new going on, theoretically, that is due to the existence of genAI, but it's also not totally false. What's at stake in what I've just discussed are the twin problems of meaning and intention as authorial-agential and the question of the possibility of recognizing the difference between human and computer language. In both cases, the major underlying issue was their boundedness to textuality. Nothing about the wave poem itself indicates that it could possibly just be a very unlikely set of marks, and the whole point of Turing's test is that you cannot tell the difference between talking to a computer or to a human. What remains, then, is the act of recognition: of texts as readable and interpretable, including interpretations themselves.

At the heart of the problem lies the question of what kind of writing literary studies writing is, how it enacts knowledge production and how whatever we do exceeds the computational. Academic writing as such, as the linguist Simon Meier-Vieracker points out, "understood as scholarly/scientific [*wissenschaftliches*] writing in institutionalized academic contexts for research and teaching is pattern-oriented to standardized," even where "creative ideas are technically central" (2024, 140, my translation). The nexus of the "technical" and the "creative" in Meier-Vieracker's words is coincidental, but nonetheless peculiarly apropos of the way recent criticism has talked about the creative work of literary studies. Perhaps most notably, Jonathan Kramnick has recently averred that literary criticism is "inescapably creative" (2023, 75)—and that it is, in a very concrete sense, also a "technē," a skill. I have already raised above the distinction made in

AI studies between "intelligence" and "skill." Skill is key to Kramnick's, but also other scholars', recent reimagining of literary studies practice. In his long essay *Criticism and Truth*, Kramnick argues that we should understand literary studies as "skilled practice" (39), where, in fact, its very nature *as* a skilled practice has "epistemic significance" (63).

Kramnick's central question is: "What do literary critics actually do when they write about texts" (22). He seeks to produce an "epistemic rationale of literary studies" (26), and finds it in the manipulation of text, specifically: in the performance of everyday practices of close reading, among them the "skilled practice" of "in-sentence quotation," which has, to him, epistemic significance. "There is knowledge that is manifest in the act of placing words just so, even as there is knowledge that comes from what one has placed" (39). Knowledge exists where scholars produce what Kramnick calls the "apt form" (40) combining their own words with those of another (the quoted author, for instance). And, in the final analysis, it is "aptness of style and dexterity of quotation [that] have epistemic significance" (46). Just to reiterate the point, because it's quite crucial to my context: Kramnick's argument throughout *Criticism and Truth* is that, to quote him quoting Ernest Sosa, the apt performance is "true because competent" (63). At the same time, this apt performance is "inescapably creative" (75); it "works with what is given, in its materials" (77) but shapes something new: criticism from literature.

This is also where the skill-ness of literary criticism resides. Kramnick approves of the distinction that the philosopher Gilbert Ryle proposes between two kinds of knowledge: "knowing that" and "knowing how," where the former is, in too simple a parsing, mainly intellectual, the second largely embodied or practical. You may, for instance, very well know that a drawer is built in this and that fashion without knowing how to do it; you may equally know how to ride a bike without knowing that these are the things you need to do to ride a bike. We might, again too simply, call these "intelligence" and "skill" aspects of knowledge, just to get the distinction clearer for my purposes here. Kramnick would like close reading, the principal interpretative practice of contemporary literary studies, understood as a learned skill, rather than a matter of (or as the only real expression of) intellectual capacity to understand literature. Understood like that, close reading's "truths would dwell in the writing itself"

(56–57).[12] Echoes of Turing's argument, for sure?[13] The interaction between skill with text and knowledge creation asks us to at least consider what it would mean for genAI to be "as good as" we are in producing literary criticism outputs. "Getting it right," says Kramnick, "is a kind of knowledge" (56), and "the veracity of any inquiry depends on how well the performance is done" (57). Like Turing's test, it's only the outcome that matters, not how you get there.

It's at least an unfortunate coincidence that Kramnick's argument straddles two moments in literary studies anxiety. What Kramnick responds to overtly is a disciplinary moment in which "some believe that the discipline has no [epistemic] rationale" (26). This moment has the well-known and oft-belabored crisis of the humanities in the background, the decline of English studies in the foreground, MINT on a continuing rise and the question of how to defend what we do on the minds of all who care for what we do. But Kramnick's defense was then published in the moment of genAI, against the background of which his arguments become at least slightly more awkward.

For Kramnick, the question of skill is, I think, implicitly invoked because it sets off literary studies practice against fields in which repeatability, strong and coherent methodologies, and the external validation of truth reign supreme. As he explicitly points out, "methods and norms suited to the sciences, including especially those of replication, don't suit the humanities" (24). And from his discussion, the skills required to perform literary studies are—echoes of the creative we've discussed already—virtually ineffable, but inescapably human. The language of "skill" implies a number of things that are important. Most vitally, it suggests that something can be learned, or at least honed, but only on the basis of an existing

[12] For this distinction and its relation to AI, see also Dreyfus (1992). Dreyfus described access to know-how, the kind of knowledge which escapes the possibility to be stated as a proposition but rather inheres, as it were, in an action itself, as a key problem for AI research—"incredibly difficult, perhaps in principle impossible, to program" (27). Importantly, however, Dreyfus's concern is for what he cites from Charles Taylor as the whole set of "situations and the possibilities" (260) that a human might find themselves in, rather than the very narrow and specific case of text generation.

[13] It may or may not be relevant that Kramnick's philosophical touchstone, Ryle, was also the author of *The Concept of Mind* (1949), in which he noted his disbelief in the possibility of a "ghost in the machine," a mechanical version of mind. As Colin Burrow points out, Turing's paper can be read in opposition to Ryle's ideas here (2019, 411); and also, less specifically, in opposition to much of current work on genAI in relation to (literary) creative imitation.

and thoroughly pre-theoretical, potentially atheoretical aptitude. This is one way in which it can be distinguished from "knowledge"—from "knowing that," at least. I know, for instance, the theoretical way to make a chest of drawers, even though I lack the skill to actually make one (like most men, however, I assume that this is largely because of my lack of power tools appropriate to the job). It also suggests an embodiment in performance unrelated to intellectual understanding. My daughter has the skill to ride a bike without understanding what she does—indeed, the miniscule movements of the hands on the handles that stabilize the bike, or the initial balancing of a yet unstable ride are, potentially, outside of intellectualization, of making conscious as knowledge, entirely. The literary scholar-craftswoman cannot be taught, as such, but only trained. "Over time, one becomes equipped with the knowledge to perform the action in a way that is adept and that seems on reflection, especially by others, to half create, half pick out features the world that are true" (25). Whatever is going on, though, the process is ineluctably human and embodied: "Knowledge resides in the fingers doing the writing as much as the eyes doing the reading" (60). The process of forming apt sentences, whose aptness is the sole arbiter of their constitution as literary studies knowledge, is a material process, one which blurs the boundaries between scholarship, art, and crafts.[14]

Without wanting to make Kramnick the arbiter of what literary studies is, his particular linkage between "skill" and "knowledge" is striking. And he is by no means alone in understanding literary studies' interpretative practice as a skilled craft and an embodied activity. Robert Eaglestone, for instance, talks about two contemporary aspects of literary studies—the "craft of metaphor spotting" and the "activity of close reading" (2019, 39). In a very similar way, the German literary scholars Steffen Martus and Carlos Spoerhase suggest that literary studies involves a process of making "fit," "*passend*" (2022, 126) without an intelligible external referent for adjudicating this fit. In the place of repeatable method, Martus and Spoerhase also see "practicing," "*einüben*," and a relationship between "master" craftsmen and "novices" (25) who, at the feet of those with a longer practice in the craft, can show—but never quite explain—the

[14] As N. Katherine Hayles points out, though, "the emphasis on individual creativity, if over-accentuated at the expense of collaboration, may tend to obscure the fact that all knowledge creation is highly collaborative because it builds on and extends what is already known" (2024, 262).

process of making literary criticism. As John Guillory notes, this is a consequence of the framing of a practice as a craft: in craft inheres the "underlying principle of transmission from one body to another, teacher to disciple" (2022, 155). In the context of their praxeology of literary studies, the actual performance of literary interpretation, the work that all our other work is ostensibly just the institutional sideshow for, takes on the same kind of mysterious quality that the creative impulse that genius have for artists elsewhere, and the transmission of this quality to others return to the pre-professional, the entirely interpersonal.

In *Professing Criticism*, John Guillory argues that the "embodied nature of this kind of [craft] knowledge is even the basis of its claim to value, if also the occasion of a certain mystification of aesthetic accomplishment" (2022, 155). This is, in many ways, the central field of tensions I am after. Departing ever so slightly from the gist of Guillory's point, I would note that it is a renewed turn we're witnessing, after a longer period in which more scientific, if you like, approaches have held sway—approaches, anyway, which have not so much focused on the practice of literary studies as on its societal aims. In the previous chapter, I linked discussions of genAI literature to specific literary studies concerns, already prevalent before genAI, about its object, "literature." In the context of literary studies, genAI is bound up in concerns, also preexisting, about the nature of the subject itself, concerns traceable at least through the so-called "method wars" (see Lanzendörfer and Nilges 2025; Lanzendörfer 2023). The discussion around versions of postcritique (Felski 2009, 2015; Anker and Felski 2019, among others) highlighted attention to less detached modes of reading as being more attentive to the quote-unquote "ordinary" modes of reading literature. In so doing, they essentially avowed a humanistic angle on literary studies criticism that, under the umbrella term of critique, it argued had evacuated these human, but also ultimately ineffable, reactions to literature that make the experience of reading matter. The specifics of this proposal matter less here than their gesture: they were meant to renew the usefulness of literary studies, gesture toward an alternative that would make it, as I've argued elsewhere, matter more by being less critical (2023, 224), but also by insisting on the centrality of the *human* experience and ineluctably human and undetached qualities. (The human, of course, here is incidental: in the heyday of postcritique, no other but the human subject was readily imaginable.) Like postcritique, recent turns to judgment in literary studies (such as Clune 2019) have sought to carve out spaces where the processes by which the discipline has previously operationalized itself are decentered. As John Guillory has recently pointed out, for instance, the disciplinary mainstay of close reading is, in effect, mainly a practice of writing that is "showing the work of reading." It does not, Guillory says, "guarantee validity in interpretation; rather, it opens interpretation to inspection and contestation by other readers" (2025, 60). But even in this limited intersubjective inspectability, it stands opposed to the movements toward personal experience and ultimately unquestionable judgment that have come to be elements of the discourse around literary studies in the past decade or two.

What unites all of these efforts, Anahid Nersessian has argued, is that they are attempts to refashion the work of literary studies that "arguably [have] less to do with the content or style of literary criticism than with the fraying of its social purpose" (2022, 181). Like the various responses from critics partial to critique, it should be said, they are attempts to carve out a space for literary studies that is both socially accepted and intellectually valid. It is in this tradition that I want to read all the practice theories of Kramnick, Martus and Spoerhase, and Guillory. In different ways, they posit the ineluctably human, but also finally slightly mysterious moment of literary studies knowledge production through the production of text as a defense of literary studies as such. In so doing, they inadvertently (one assumes) return us to the previous moment in which creativity was invoked—indeed, in which it was first conceived. Samuel Franklin points out that what "really lay behind the sudden interest in research on creativity" in the 1950s and 1960s "was an anxiety about the nature of white-collar work, particularly among scientists and technicians." The call to understand one's work as creative helped to "model oneself not on the machine but on the artist or the poet. It was to pursue work with an intrinsic motivation, a passion for the act of creation. It was to be more *human*" (2023, 15). Somewhat coincidentally, this description of how creativity came to be foregrounded in non-manual labor appears tailor-made, also, to evade the challenge of genAI.

I want to be clear here that I am not criticizing any of the argument about either the importance of understanding critical method or the belief in the creativity of literary studies practices. In fact, I am largely sympathetic to both points, though I quibble with details of Kramnick's analysis. What interests me here is the upshot of Kramnick's argument for the moment of genAI. Perhaps inadvertently, the advocates of understanding literary studies as a craft seek to carve out a specific place for the discipline, most especially one where it should be granted time and resources to enable to kind of on-the-job training that the various kinds of neoliberal assaults on the university, in the form of high tuition cost or post-Bologna education reforms, have made increasingly impossible. Craft can work only where there is time for showing, for experiencing, for understanding in the process of making—less a matter of following repeatable instructions as a matter of experiencing the process of making. What unites these calls to understand literary studies as craft, then, is an understanding that, were literary studies more properly recognized as a craft, it would also need to be accepted as of a different order from the sciences, freer, more time-consuming, more human.[15]

In the moment of genAI, however, this becomes strikingly problematical. Guillory highlights the difficulty of the move toward craft even absent the existence of genAI, and in general terms: "Those seeking to professionalize any particular occupation must persuade potential clients that their occupational expertise is more than craft, sometimes by derogating the very craft practice upon which professions are often based" (2022, 20). And under the regime of genAI, we're suddenly exposed to an awkward double bind. The (already tenuous) route of escape from the threat of genAI creativity tends to be, as I've said, a denial of its capacity for creativity on the grounds of its lack of intelligence, understood as an exclusively human domain, and mere skill. In Kramnick et al.'s understanding, skill, alas, is exactly what literary studies practices are all about. Kramnick, Martus, and Spoerhase seem to preempt at least some of this problem by their insistence on the embodiedness of the skilled activity: Kramnick's insistence that "knowledge resides in the fingers doing the writing as much as the eyes doing the reading" (2022, 60) suggests, on the one hand, a somewhat unwarranted proximity between the activities of weaving words just so and, say, weaving reeds just so. In the latter case, yes, the dexterity of the fingers matters; in the former, alas, it does not. My insights into *Moby Dick* are exactly as valuable typed by two fingers on a keyboard as by ten, exactly as valuable handwritten as dictated. On the other hand, Kramnick's insistence, wrong as it is, is now perhaps best read as a preemptive defense against encroaching genAI. For, if manual dexterity mattered, we would be well within our rights to dismiss genAI, whose textual dexterity isn't matched by any manual dexterity. Recall the point

[15] In their recent handbook on close reading, Dan Sinykin and Johanna Winant (2025) curiously appear to split the difference, arguing for both a Kramnick-inspired craft aspect for close reading and providing a near-algorithmic five-step program for such a close reading.

raised above by the Google researcher François Chollet (2019) about genAI's skill versus its intelligence. Invoking "craft" as the measure of skill is an accidentally clever way to translate ineffable creativity—which does not seem to be, as I've been at pains to argue, in principle occluded to genAI—into a material register that is. "Craft" invokes, at once, suitability for purpose, the imperfection of human endeavor, and non-mechanical irrepeatability, all of which appear to escape the computational altogether. Skill and intelligence now both become human domains, and there's no more room for genAI practice in literary studies.

Again: the relationship between the various practice theory versions of literary studies epistemology are accidentally related to genAI, but instructive. In tying our work's epistemology assertively to how it is done and insisting that this specific how is finally situated in an unrationalizable, unoperationalizable creative realm, they open up a defense against genAI so long as we are agreed that the qualities they insist are human are, in fact, absolutely human. And it ultimately pays, I think, to doubt both of these premises: absolutely human creativity, and the epistemological primacy of the act of writing, tied as they are.

Close reading's epistemology, following from Guillory, centers on performance, yes, on the work of reading, presented in the form of writing. It is, in fact, readers, we might say with Kramnick, who get to judge the "aptness" of the work shown and decide whether or not, therefore, it has produced knowledge—not, as in Kramnick's parsing, some mysterious, extra-readerly aptness as such. And this is, in the age of genAI, where the anxiety for us lies.[16] There is a surprising dearth of discussion about what counts as "knowledge" in literary studies, it bears pointing out, a problem related to the larger question that René van Woudenberg has identified: that despite much attention, especially in hermeneutical philosophy, to the question of interpretation, the relation between interpretation and knowledge has not received sustained attention (2019, 4–6). We may well, as Woudenberg himself says, doubt that the kinds of interpretations we generally count as professional interpretations, for instance, Marxist readings of *Moby Dick*, "constitute knowledge or reach the high epistemic status of

[16] The most extreme version of this anxiety is noted by Holly Dugan and Dolsy Smith: the "fears that knowledge itself, at least as practiced in the academy, can 'no longer [be] operated and mediated by language *as such*' (according to Kirschenbaum and Raley)" (2024, 519). Kirschenbaum and Raley explicitly limit their argument to "leading science and technologies" (2024, 508) and Dugan and Smith somewhat anxiously extend this to "knowledge" *tout court*.

being beyond reasonable doubt" (223). For my purposes here, indeed, I am only interested in literary studies knowledge to point out that whatever the status of interpretation epistemologically might be argued to be, its claim to knowledge, following Kramnick, is not one that could be validated text-externally. It is necessarily bound up in how you make the argument, textually.

And, perhaps more forcefully: whatever we call our interpretations, even if we call them knowledge, they are never more than plausible readings.[17] I have repeatedly suggested above that literary studies epistemology deals in plausibility, rather than empirical and externally verifiable truths, certainly in the context of our interpretative work.[18] Key to the question of plausibility in literary studies as I understand it here is that it is entirely social, entirely professional in nature—an expression of what, in one recent investigation, the literary critics Dan Sinykin and Johanna Winant dub "our rules" (2025, 16). It is not, as in most discussions of plausibility (see for instance Poston 2024), tied to observable or experientially available (in terms I used above: world-related) events or states. Instead, it is intersubjectively validated by its acceptance as plausible by the community of our peers, which in turn draws on textual work to adjudicate this plausibility—our own senses of the text, combined with our previous readings on it. As Simone Winko and her colleagues note, plausibility is "a predicate that is ascribed not to facts or events but to certain kinds of statements and systems of statements" (2024, 38). We adjudicate the plausibility of a statement about a literary text in various ways: by finding the statement to be well-reasoned, collectively accepted, or fitting to already accepted statements, for instance. Plausibility is, Winko et al. argue, a minimal standard of literary studies acceptability; stronger ways of thinking about literary interpretation's statements are imaginable, up to and including their "truth"; but, at a minimum, we expect literary interpretation to fulfill the criterion of plausibility.

In Winko et al.'s parsing of the term, plausibility is "not concentrated merely on the justification of an argument, but can also consider, through

[17] I discuss this question elsewhere at greater length (Lanzendörfer, forthcoming-a, forthcoming-b), where I develop a partially theoretical, partially instrumental proposal to understand literary studies interpretations as knowledge.

[18] A related term here is Hans-Georg Gadamer's "evident," which in the original German is "einleuchtend." For Gadamer, the "evident has not been proved and is not absolutely certain, but it asserts itself by reason of its own merit within the realm of the possible and probable" (2004, 479). See also Roach, Monot and Lanzendörfer (forthcoming).

the aspects of internal coherence or fitness and of collective acceptance, the dimension of scholarly-scientific presentation: this presentation is key to the argumentative context and participates in the possibility of identifying a coherent argument" (40). Winko et al., in other words, understand plausibility as the epistemological category which names what Kramnick calls "aptness." As a category, it is both free from a world-relation (except mediatedly, through what they dub previously-accepted statements) but explicitly bound up in reception and rhetoric.

What should emerge from this complex of parallels, ongoing thinking about literary studies practices and epistemologies, is that our work emerges only in the act of its reception—not, I think, in the sense in which reader-response critics from Iser to Fish had it, but in the simpler sense that Kramnick's apt is an apt his professional reader adjudicates (as in peer review). Its plausibility inheres in the ability of the writing to convince, not in the intellectual effort itself. As Ted Poston puts it: "To the extent that a claim is not rationally surprising, given the evidence, it is plausible" (2024). Surprise, as postcritics have been at pains to point out, appears to lie entirely in the domain of the reader. And plausibility, in turn, is exactly the frame of reference through which genAI text production is best read—for better or worse. At a higher order, as Jin, Li, and Hamarneh point out, "plausibility is the most widespread concept" in AI studies to judge the value of an explanation for AI's reasoning (2023, 2); at a lower order, it is the central category through which we make both *ad hoc*, but also more durable decisions about the kinds of outputs we receive from our engagements with genAI *tout court*. Plausibility is the category which produces genAI hallucinations, too, as OpenAI researchers aver: "hallucinations are plausible but false statements" (Kalai et al. 2025). In all of these cases, plausibility describes a relationship between the text and the world it references. In the case of explainable AI, the textual evidence AI gives about its own workings cannot be verified in the first place; in the case of hallucinations, it can in principle be verified but, textually, does not look out of place. Both cases describe a negative correlation, of course; but this is merely the flipside of genAI's ability to produce plausibility otherwise, plausibility that, it bears stressing, epistemologically is little different from the plausible textual arguments that we produce in our writing practice.

The thought that our writing, as a practice, matters is not unique to literary studies, of course. In his defense of human creative writing that I have been stringing you along with, Ted Chiang points to a moment he says many novelists will have experienced: the moment when someone comes up to them with an idea for a novel and expects the author to write that novel, for a share of the profits. As Chiang notes, "such a person inadvertently reveals that they think formulating sentences is a nuisance rather than a fundamental part of storytelling in prose" (2024, 7). But Chiang, it seems to me, is mistaken in this. "Formulating sentences" is not a fundamental part of storytelling, except in so far as it is necessary precondition like "being alive": *having formulated* sentences, on the other hand, are (those that will be read). How these sentences ultimately got to be on the page will remain opaque to readers, professional or not. Likewise, it seems to me Kramnick is wrong in the analogous formulation he offers for literary studies: that there is "knowledge that is manifest in the act of placing words just so." Maybe not so much wrong as unhelpfully fixated on the solitary scholar's activity. More correct, I think, to say that "there is knowledge manifest in the words *placed* just so"—but then, of course, whoever or whatever placed the words just so does not matter anymore.

In that epistemological situation, however, we are no longer different from genAI. How the words got there does not matter. Now, to be sure: if knowledge were indeed manifest in the act of placing words just so, we would just be back at the Turing test, and already, we would find ourselves struggling to distance ourselves as human literary scholars from genAI encroachment. The point, though, is more urgently that Kramnick is *already* wrong: the best category we have to adjudicate anything like validity in interpretation, plausibility, resides not in the act of placing, but in the communal, intersubjective act of reading. How the words got on the page also doesn't matter for your publication record in *New Literary History* or the *New Left Review*. It doesn't matter if you *understand* anything about Marxism, or anything else, for that matter. What matters *at most* is the plausibility of your sentences: whether or not you're read as having understood Marxism (to the extent, that is, that your reviewers have understood it and are willing to resist you). Now, clearly, you may be able to emulate a plausible Marxist reading of *Moby Dick* because you genuinely *are* an expert in Marxism and have genuinely come up with good ideas about *Moby Dick*. I'm not saying that all performance of expertise is always only emulation of expertise, or that all emulation of expertise by non-experts will always go undetected. I'm merely pointing out that, for successful attempts at emulation, you (by definition) are not able to tell the difference between emulation and genuine expertise.

What's the upshot of all this? Literary studies has for some time been waging a defensive struggle, one centered around rethinking what its purpose and practices are. These struggles have been ongoing for almost two decades, and genAI's arrival comes at their tail-end, at a moment when, quite by coincidence, much effort has already been expanded on, as it were, humanizing the discipline. What genAI reveals to us, again quite coincidentally, is that very little about these efforts have actually named either uniquely human qualities or fully grappled with the upshot of their constitution in text. GenAI points us, more fully than any previous challenge to the then-prevailing orthodoxies about literary studies, to this fact: that the most important category by which we adjudicate the validity of any interpretation is the plausibility of its textual formation. And, unfortunately for us, this plausibility cannot reasonably be asserted to be a causal of the manual dexterity of the writer, their intelligence, or some other quality inhering in their humanity; we merely thought we could do that, because there were no other writers.

Let me be clear again about my claims: I'm not saying genAI is, or can be, doing exactly the same thing as a literary scholar, except when I *am* saying that it is. I'm with Pierre-Héli Monot when he notes that humans have been especially resistant to acknowledging the "humanness" of those qualities in machines that are most strongly shared between us and them. The node of "skill" that links what current gen AI in fact does (maybe it is A.S. Byatt after all—"artificial skill" rather than artificial intelligence) and what we've come to see as the specific quality of literary criticism's practice is more than just suggestive here. It is no mere rhetoric that in the most recent developments of language-driven, prompted agential models of AI, "skill" has emerged as a key term. In Anthropic's diction, "skills" package "your expertise into composable resources," and building a "skill" is "like putting together an onboard guide for a new hire" (2025)—or, in our context, new literary scholars. "Skill," in other words, emerges (for Anthropic, anyway) as a matter not of ineffably human iteration on learned behavior, but rather as a more complex version of run-of-the-mill prompt engineering. The confluence of these terms, the way in which our efforts at outlining the specialness of literary studies finds itself almost immediately confronted with assertions of its utter lack of specialness: these are a challenge to think again, and possibly a bit harder, about how we imagine our work, and how we're under threat, as professionals, by genAI. And by extension: what it would mean for the significance of our work if, in fact, it just could be done by AI.

References

Alberto, Isabelle Rose, et al. 2025. The Rise of 'Vibe Science': How AI Threatens Scientific Rigor. *TechRxiv.org*. Online.

Anker, Elizabeth, and Rita Felski, eds. 2019. *Critique and Postcritique*. Durham: Duke University Press.

Anthropic. 2025. Equipping Agents for the Real World with Agent Skills. Online.

Bajohr, Hannes. 2023. When in Doubt, Go to the Beach. In *Again Theory: A Forum on Language, Meaning, and Intent in a Time of Stochastic Parrots*.

Bajohr, Hannes. 2024. On Artificial and Post-artificial Texts: Machine Learning and the Reader's Expectations of Literary and Non-literary writing. In *The AI Revolution: Speculations on Authorship, Pedagogy, and the Future of the Profession*, edited by Nir Evron and Roi Tortakovsky. Special Issue of *Poetics Today* 45 (2): 331–361.

Binder, Jeffrey M. 2022. *Language and the Rise of the Algorithm*. Chicago: University of Chicago Press.

Castelvecchi, Davide. 2025. DeepMind and OpenAI Models Solve Maths Problems at Level of Top Students. *Nature*, July 24. Online.

Catani, Stephanie, ed. 2023. *Handbuch Künstliche Intelligenz und die Künste*. Berlin: DeGruyter.

Chiang, Ted. 2024. Why A.I. Isn't Going to Make Art. *The New Yorker*, August 31. Online.

Chollet, François. 2019. On the Measure of Intelligence. *arXiv.org*. Online.

Clune, Michael. 2019. *A Defense of Judgment*. Chicago: University of Chicago Press.

Da, Nan Z. 2025. Literary Criticism in the Age of AI. *New Left Review* 155: 103–127, September/October 2025.

Dreyfus, Hubert L. 1992. *What Computers Still Can't Do*. Cambridge: MIT Press.

Dugan, Holly, and Dolsy Smith. 2024. Untimely Models. *PMLA* 139 (3): 516–521.

Felski, Rita. 2009. *The Uses of Literature*. New York: Wiley.

Felski, Rita. 2015. *The Limits of Critique*. Chicago: University of Chicago Press.

Evron, Nir. 2024. LLMs and the Amazing Shrinking University. In *The AI Revolution: Speculations on Authorship, Pedagogy, and the Future of the Profession*, edited by Nir Evron and Roi Totakovsky, 317–324. Special Issue of *Poetics Today* 45 (2).

Foucault, Michel. 1998/1969. What is an Author? In *Aesthetics, Method, and Epistemology*, 205–222. New York: The New Press.

Franklin, Samuel. 2023. *The Cult of Creativity: A Surprisingly Recent History*. Chicago: University of Chicago Press.

Gadamer, Hans-Georg. 2004. *Truth and Method*. London: Routledge.

Gil, Alex. 2023. On the Uses of Text beyond Intention. In *Again Theory: A Forum on Language, Meaning, and Intent in a Time of Stochastic Parrots* (blog), edited by Matthew Kirschenbaum, June 28. Online.

Guillory, John. 2022. *Professing Criticism: Essays on the Organization of Literary Study*. Chicago: University of Chicago Press.

Guillory, John. 2025. *On Close Reading*. Chicago and London: University of Chicago Press.

Hayles, N. Katherine. 2024. Don't Ban AI From Your Writing Classroom; Require It! *Poetics Today* 45 (2): 259–265.

Hayot, Eric. 2014. Academic Writing, I Love You. I Really Do. *Critical Inquiry* 41 (1): 53–77.

Lanzendörfer, Tim. forthcoming-a. The Labor of Literary Studies.

Lanzendörfer, Tim. forthcoming-b. What Does Literary Studies Know?

Heaven, Will Douglas. 2023. Google DeepMind Used a Large Language Model to Solve an Unsolved Math Problem. *MIT Technology Review*. Online.

Jin, Weina, Xiaoxiao Li, and Ghassan Hamarneh. 2023. Why is Plausibility Surprisingly Problematic as an XAI Criterion? *arXiv.org*. Online.

Juhl, Peter. 1981. *Interpretation: An Essay in the Philosophy of Literary Criticism*. Princeton: Princeton University Press.

Kalai, Adam Tauman, Ofir Nachum, Santosh S. Vempala, and Edwin Zhang. 2025. Why Language Models Hallucinate. *arXiv:org*. Online.

Kirschenbaum, Matthew, and Rita Raley. 2024. AI and the University as a Service. *PMLA* XXX:1–12.

Knapp, Steven, and Walter Benn Michaels. 1982. Against Theory. *Critical Inquiry* 8 (4): 723–742.

Knapp, Steven, and Walter Benn Michaels. 2023. Here is a Wave Poem that I Wrote…I Hope You Like It! In *Again Theory: A Forum on Language, Meaning, and Intent in a Time of Stochastic Parrots*, edited by Matthew Kirschenbaum. *Critical Inquiry*, Online.

Konstantinou, Lee. 2025. Peer Review Paranoia. *The Chronicle of Higher Education*, September 2. Online.

Kramnick, Johnathan. 2023. *Criticism and Truth*. Chicago: University of Chicago Press.

Kwa, Thomas, et al. 2025. Measuring AI Ability to Complete Long Tasks. *arXiv.org*. Online.

Lanzendörfer, Tim. 2023. The Work of Literary Studies: Interpretation, Argument, and Socioaesthetic Experience. In *Futures of Literary Studies*, edited by Mathias Nilges and Tim Lanzendörfer. Special issue of *Textual Practice* 37 (2): 221–239.

Lanzendörfer, Tim, and Mathias Nilges. 2025. Preface: Futures of Literary Studies, Revisited. In *Futures of Literary Studies*, edited by Mathias Nilges and Tim Lanzendörfer, x–xiii. Cham: Palgrave Macmillan.

Martus, Steffen, and Carlos Spoerhase. 2022. *Geistesarbeit. Eine Praxeologie der Geisteswissenschaften*. Frankfurt: Suhrkamp.

Meier-Vieracker, Simon. 2024. Uncreative Academic Writing: Sprachtheoretische Überlegungen zu Künstlicher Intelligenz in der akademischen Textproduktion. In *KI:Text. Diskurse über KI-Textgeneratoren*, edited by Gerhard Schreiber and Lukas Ohly, 133–144. Berlin: DeGruyter.

Monot, Pierre-Héli. 2023. Robopathen und Robopathinnen aller Länder…wenn die KI die Drehbücher schreibt. *Merkur* 903:84–92.
Nersessian, Anahid. 2022. For Love of Beauty? Literary Criticism in Troubled Times. *New Left Review* 133/134:179–196.
Perlow, Seth. 2024. Generative Theories, Pretrained Responses: Large AI Models and the Humanities. *PMLA* 139 (3): 548–522.
Poston, Ted. 2024. Experience, Plausibility, and Evidence. *Philarchive.org.*
Putnam, Hilary. 1981. *Reason, Truth, and History.* Cambridge: Cambridge University Press.
Reisner, Alex. 2025. Search LibGen, the Pirated-Books database That Meta Used to Train AI. *The Atlantic*. Online.
Roach, Rebecca, Pierre-Héli Monot, and Tim Lanzendörfer. forthcoming. The Plausibility of Academic Forms in the Age of their Computational Reproducibility. Under review.
Schmidt, Paul G., and Amnon J. Meir. 2023. Using Generative AI for Literature Searches and Scholarly Writing: Is the Integrity of Scientific Discourse in Jeopardy? *arXiv.org*. Online.
Schüttpelz, Erhard. 2023. *Deutland.* Berlin: Matthes & Seitz.
Sinkyin, Dan, and Johanna Winant, eds. 2025. *Close Reading for the 21st Century.* Princeton: Princeton University Press.
Slocombe, Will, and Genevieve Lively, eds. 2024. *The Routledge Handbook of AI and Literature.* London: Routledge.
Van Woudenberg, René. 2019. *The Epistemology of Reading and Interpretation.* Cambridge: Cambridge University Press.
Winko, Simone, et al. 2024. *Praktiken des Plausibilisierens. Untersuchungen zum Argumentieren in literaturwissenschaftlichen Interpretationstexten.* Göttingen: Universitätsverlag Göttingen.
Zeraoulia, Rafik. 2025. Why Mathematicians Resist AI: Between Rigor, Risk, and Opportunity. *ArXiv.org*. Online.

CHAPTER 4

By Way of Ending: Some Value(s) of Literary Studies

Abstract The conclusion explores, in a tentative and polemic fashion, some of the imaginable consequences of understanding genAI as potentially capable of doing the textual work of literary studies, specifically: that of interpretation. It begins from a discussion of whether it makes sense to carve out moments of exceptionality from a generalizable sense of literary studies writing as pedestrian. It suggests the links this discussion has with concerns over publish-or-perish ideologies and ultimately suggests that the fundamental question here is simply: what do we think literary studies is good for? Exploring potential consequences of genAI to literary studies, as well as the longer connections this discussion has with some ongoing re-evaluations of the field, it finally suggests that what emerges as a viable future of literary studies is a reorientation away from producing outputs toward a training of students and of wider society in the practices of close reading and interpretation.

Keywords Literary studies • Literary theory • Creativity • Literary sociology • Artificial intelligence • Literature • Craft • Skill • Interpretation • Close reading

This little book is concerned with two, at best three problems: how to relate to imaginable genAI literature that is indistinguishable as text from

T. Lanzendörfer, *AI and the Challenge to Literary Studies*,
https://doi.org/10.1007/978-3-032-25526-6_4

human writing; and more importantly, how to relate to imaginable genAI literary studies that is indistinguishable as text from human writing—what the overall impact, then, of genAI on the profession could be. It has suggested that these are crucial questions in light of recent discussions of the structure and purpose of literary studies as well as genAI. But one thing it's not yet done is suggest what follows, at least not in a sustained fashion, both for our actual practice and the idea we have of our discipline's value. I want to end with a couple of consequences that I can see that stem from the problems I'm suggesting genAI poses—not exactly solutions, admittedly, but gestures toward them, and if not exactly assertions of value, then at least an idea of how to think about them.

Recall this book's opening with a game of Go. The reason for starting out with this scene was to introduce a number of key terms I've now pursued throughout, but also to suggest that it may not pay dividends to ignore the possibility that our most cherished intellectual achievements—whether we're Go players or literary critics—may be reproduced computationally. This explicitly includes, in literary studies and probably the humanities writ large, the "kind of intellectual work that changes the conversation, opens new horizons, circumvents outdated puzzles, or opens up new ones" (Evron 2024, 322). It's relatively easy to reject even the possibility that on this exalted field, there might be trouble brewing. When it comes to the "horizon-expanding work that is the holy grail of our profession," Nir Evron avers, LLMs "do not yet pose a real threat and perhaps never will." That's because, Evron says, it is fundamentally different from simple "reorganization of facts or deft manipulation of massive stores of information. It is its ability to induce a Gestalt shift in its readers, one that brings new truth candidates, avenues of research, and problems into view" (322) that sets human work apart from even imaginable genAI work. There's something ineffable about this list—and we've encountered this ineffability before, with different terms—something that foregrounds an almost mystical essence to truly creative work that is not reducible (though Evron usefully hedges his bets) to computation. Because computers can't come up with strokes of genius, although, of course, as the opening anecdote of this book shows, that is more matter of what you call "genius" than anything else.

What echoes through Evron's take on post-AI literary studies is a hopefulness about the future of the discipline that other writers on genAI's present in the discipline have also hinted at. Like Evron, Katherine Elkins suggests the possibility that the "postlabor" utopian promise of genAI's ascent "could be a return to the 'uselessness' of the humanities" in which we avoid the "neocapitalist [sic?] imperative for utility" (2024, 563). While there might be fewer of us (because all the "rote academic articles," as Evron has it, needn't be written anymore), those that remain might have more time to think, to work, to produce the genuine shifts in understanding the world and ourselves that humanities work strives for. Happy as that sounds, it's also, as Matteo Pasquinelli's (2023) recent work shows, a common pipedream generally evoked by technological innovators at every step in processes of automation. Machines will free your time is a commonplace ideologeme frequently flanked by assertions as to how this technological disruption will be different from the last. The advent of the digital computer radically freed human computers from their utility, yes, because it eliminated what Marx and Engels called their "exclusive sphere of activity" (2010, 47). It also radically freed them from their livelihoods. It bears saying that, somewhat paradoxically, it is our own objectified labor—all of our previous literary studies work, now data training sets for LLMs—that genAI returns into the new automated process of genAI literary studies in which we would no doubt like to continue to sell our living labor. In our case, though, since we are not making cheaper brushes or coats, or even whatever false need contemporary capitalism imposes on us, the question would be: why should anybody buy? Is there a space for artisanal literary studies and its hand-crafted, mind-crafted outputs, and if so—why, and who for? What is the nature of literary studies ability to change the world's *Gestalt*—where does it reside—or is it, perhaps, mostly a way of changing the discipline's own *Gestalt*? Even if we thought we could change the world: in order to make the idea that the kind of rarefied existence sketched above is even vaguely plausible, we would have to exempt the university from the logics of neoliberal capitalism, in what appears to be a fairly bold move. Or we have to suggest that the real "value-creating power of individual labor" (Marx 1973, 694) manifests itself not in the mass or scale of outputs, but in their quality and, as noted, needs to be grounded in something ineffably human that thereby exceeds the capacity of artificial, generative "intelligence." This is, as we have seen, a common move in the creative fields of literary writing and literary studies, but it is also desperate and potentially fatal if, as at least it stands within the realm of possibility, there is in fact nothing necessary about the human element in the production of either sensitive literature or culturally sensitive criticism. Alas: there's currently exactly as much evidence for the proposition that genAI's textual outputs may eventually resemble our most "horizon-expanding" work as for the obverse case. And, more to the point, most of our work is not horizon-expanding in the first place, as Evron points out. In arguing from the baseline of the best and brightest that's ever been put to paper, as we have seen, literary theorists such as Jonathan Kramnick and genAI scholars such as Evron, even when they acknowledge Sturgeon's law that 90% of everything is crud, cannot quite let go of the remaining 10%—indeed, valorize it as what we should hold up as the best, perhaps the only meaningful, literary studies work. But I think that the answers they produce as to how we manage the current and impending crises of literary studies are incomplete because of their willingness to carve out a special place for human achievement, valued by us, valuable to society, validated by society as a value to it. The offer on the table, in Evron's and Elkins's parsing both, is the rarefied exercise of judgment, the occasional production of a handwrought uniquity, at best the intercession to unjam the smooth operation of the new machine—the new literary critic "supervises and guards against interruption" (Marx 1973, 692), nothing more. But we currently have no good answer to the question of what any of that might be for. If genAI comes for our sphere—our job of being "critical critics," if you like—it will not produce sphere-limited communism, but replacement, or, in the worst case, simple elimination for lack of a sense of what we're valuable for.

There's an over-quoted argument in the seventh chapter of *Capital*: "what distinguishes the worst architect from the best of bees is that the architect builds the cell in his mind before he constructs it in wax." The human architect exhibits a "purposeful will" and exercises the "free play of his own physical and mental powers"—the bee merely follows its instincts. What is distinctive about human labor is its imaginative quality, and that "the will be steadily in consonance with his purpose" (Marx 1990, 284). The unalienated laborer of this opening gambit draws on a full range of faculties—"arms and legs, head and hands" in the process of changing the external world, and his own nature at the same time.

For Marx, the point of this opening is to note that unalienated labor must have a purpose, must engage the laborer wholesale, must understand him in his quality as a human, not just as a human resource. I would wager that I am not completely alone in understanding already the alienation of my own labor, and I am certainly not alone in a utopian longing to see genAI as a way out of this state—a way to free myself from the everyday to try and achieve something great. The kicker for me right now may be that neither the state of unalienated being nor, for that matter, the potential fact that humans build in the mind first says anything at all about the quality of the final product. In fact, as Marx points out, it's very well possible that the bee's hexagon end up in all manner superior to that of man.

What distinguishes the worst literary scholar from the best of genAIs is this, that the worst literary scholar...well, that's the point, right? Given all I've said so far, I suppose we should actually be worried about what it would mean for genAI to produce literary studies that puts to shame—indeed, merely to generally reproduce in quality—what many a human literary scholar constructs. Imagine for a moment that world in which, as Seth Perlow had it, genAI solves "the problem of quantity" in output—here, in literary studies outputs. Solves, in other words, the problem that there is a finite number of literary scholars working on a vast number of texts, texts that multiply at a far greater rate than literary studies professors and their time for research do. As with literature, our problem is not, and hasn't been, too little literary studies, it is too much: too much new research already, too little time to read it, too much new literature to think about, too little time to do it. What would happen in a world in which genAI could deal with that output for us—address all of it, work on all of it, be fed with all of it? Produce our outputs, even as it consumed all of our outputs? The sad fact may be that this is not at all a solution to anything, least of all "the problem of quantity," because it might just reveal that this whole thing, our work on literature, is all a bit pointless.

The problem of quantity is, among other things, a consequence of the underlying logic of humanities career making: publish or perish, which, at the very least, is a powerful story we all tell ourselves about the nature of academic work and life (see Knöchelmann 2024). No matter that, in the current climate, it looks more like publish and perish; against the backdrop of current publication regimes in the humanities, genAI's promise of sped-up outputs takes on a curious double valence. Were it reducible, delimitable, access-restricted—could you be sure that you were the only user of Claude, what a leg up it would give you! Enhanced productivity would enable you to do more with less time, perhaps you might even be able to use to your advantage the LLMs an overworked editor could employ to ease their own troubles of finding elusive reviews (see Collu et al. 2025). But of course, it is not delimitable: everyone will have access in the same way, provided they can spend the money.

As Marcel Knöchelmann has pointed out, "publishing is, first and foremost, a formal requirement" in the contemporary academic system, rather than, for instance, actually a thing conducted with the aim to "communicate" (2024, 6).[1] That is to say, it is not so much a matter of advancing any particular set of knowledge or offering up an insight for debate; rather, publishing is a "way forward" (6), a goal to reach and a concrete thing to measure your work by. In this sense, genAI irrupts into the publication regime of the contemporary humanities with the fundamental question: if I'm already not communicating anything that I think is important, then why can't something else do that for me? And, conversely, if the mere act of publication is no longer a sign of being on a forward trajectory, what is the point of publication? You will hear the echoes of what we have already discussed above: is the point, then, to wait until you genuinely have something to communicate? To say only the most important, the most vital things? As above so here: I doubt it. And not just because it remains unclear what the most important things that could be said even are.

Because here, as above, the question remains: why should we assume that these important and vital things, even if we can come up with them, are something that genAI will be waiting for us to produce? In a recent essay, Nan Z. Da suggests a point that is, it should be clear, very close to my own thinking: "'AI' is a true forcing move for cultural and intellectual work—and for literary criticism in particular—because it forces us to go back to our foundations and define precisely what kind of humane intelligence we can offer, at our best" (106). But instead of doing that—instead of genuinely asking what we offer—she concludes her essay by an assertion

[1] Anecdotally, this seems to be the unquestioned premise even beyond the stage at which it is possible to easily "perish" in the system. I've heard from tenured colleagues that they appreciate genAI as a way to do a number of their jobs more easily. Some, like coming up with key terms for their essays, or writing standardized student emails, seem fairly innocuous. Others, however, like the prompting of genAI for article ideas, are just plain weird. Having been asked to contribute to a special issue, edited collection, or similar project by a colleague, instead of acknowledging that they have nothing to say—nothing to communicate—these colleagues prefer to communicate what genAI suggests to them, though then in their own words, so their extra-scholarly—namely their social—commitments to their colleagues do not suffer. Implicitly, at least, what these colleagues acknowledge is the limited added utility of their own thinking, and/or possibly the limited value of edited collections with invited participants.

In light of this, it's perhaps also worth pointing out that it's very likely to be us who cripple the discipline in the long-run, not genAI companies. If there's no real money in publishing—so that there's very little incentive to go full-bore into literature production—there's obviously even less money in literary studies. Nobody will *invest* in replacing us but we ourselves.

that seems, in its implications, fantastically overblown. Not only does she assert that we "know" (rather than hold dear the thought that, believe, or are institutionally bound to think) that literary criticism "cannot be an in interpretative free-for-all or just statistically approximated hearsay." She also appears to suggest that there is a link, "downstream consequences of faked comprehension," between what we do as literary critics (of Emily Dickinson poems, in her examples) and "people's bodies and lives" (127). How? It's not clear. But it's an article of faith we're familiar with: our work matters, or must matter—and, again, it matters as interpretations, as outputs. GenAI problematizes this very issue for us: it asks us what the *point* of our outputs is. It asks us if producing more outputs means having more knowledge; it asks us what would happen if we didn't need to produce outputs anymore. Against the utopian hope that it will free us to pursue something significant, it sets the stark *topos* of our current professionalism, in which we generally (apparently-obviously) don't ask ourselves this question. Thus, in the genAI moment, defenses of literary studies as a significant, useful practice collide with the revelation that, in fact, we *actually* hope to not have to do it—or not have to do it as much.

I return to the question of our outputs and our purpose at the very end of this section. For now, let me briefly take stock of a more immediate set of problems we are confronted with as a discipline. There are, again, two dimensions to the issue I want to address here: the way we relate, as a discipline, to genAI literature, and the way we relate, as a discipline, to genAI literary studies. What positions are available to us with regard to them? How should we react, how could we react, to the existence of either? Let's start with one obvious way of going forward. There is one perfectly normal and perfectly simple solution. We can do what we, as humans, habitually do with major problems: ignore them and hope they go away. Given the vagaries of genAI's futures, that hope is not even absolutely farfetched, because it actually might go away. We really just can't tell. But as with all other problems, it doesn't seem particularly wise to just ignore it, merely on the possibly off chance that, after all, all genAI's dread promises come to pass.

Let me start then, with the fairly well-trodden field of what we should do, what we can do, with genAI literature. N. Katherine Hayles formulates a version of the question like this: With "the essays, letters, short stories, poems, parodies, and even novels [produced by genAI], literary critics are confronted with a fundamental problem: should one ignore the fact that these are linguistic artifacts produced by a machine, or should that be taken into account" (2022, 643–644). In asking the question in this fashion, Hayles assumes that such a differentiation is always easily possible, presumably through paratextual information.

For Hayles, we might say, literary studies approaches to genAI texts effectively produce a cultural studies of genAI's life-worlds—"meanings specific to its capabilities and frames of reference" (2022, 653). Given Hayles's penchant to anthropomorphize genAI, her easy use of terms such as "knowledge," "awareness," or "experience" when it comes to naming what the relationship of genAI to its inputs and outputs is, this is not as surprising as it might be. But it is still wrong to simply posit even rhetorical equivalence between the kinds of exhibitions of what would, in a human, be considered knowledge, and what emerges in genAI's language work. Like many scholars of genAI, Hayles—because that is all she can do—extrapolates from linguistic expression to mind, from complexity of language use to sentience. Whether or not there is "psychological reasoning" (661) is—shades of Wittgenstein—ultimately impossible to separate from the external expression of reasoning, an external expression which in Hayles's case and mine takes the shape of text (but could also be an image or a video). Thus far, obviously, I agree. But if we do know that something is genAI generated, we may still feel free to reject it as an object of interest, simply because we can then tell that its simulation of experience is just that. Or we do so because, as humans, we are actually not that interested in the "meanings specific" to AI's "frames of reference." We could just decide we're not very interested in what genAI "thinks" in terms of literature.

So if we do not just ignore the problem of genAI literature, and hope it goes away, there are still two fairly basic solutions: we can decide, as a field, and for purely pragmatic reasons, to only do our work on human writing. We'd need to find out, or "know," that the text we discuss has been written by an actual, living, flesh-and-blood human, of course; perhaps we would do so in much the same way as we do currently already with other identitarian categories. The problem with even discussing readers' reactions to genAI literary production, as I have pointed out above, is a problem of textuality and its capacity to inform us of the humanity of the author. In fact, we can't reasonably insist that we will always know anything about a text's human origins from the text itself. So we would need to turn to extratextual means of establishing genAI authorship. We'd rely on publishers' honesty in reporting their authors as human or not; we'd rely on authors' self-identification as human; and we'd end up having similar debates around what it means not to write from lived experience, from embodied identity, and to fake or pretend to any of these, if we encountered instances of genAI passing for human as today we do when we encounter, say, writers inhabiting ethnic voices not their own.[2] This is a pragmatic if basically flawed way to adopt solutions we've always used anyway. We just add a first-order category (human/not human) that needs to be controlled for before we can do anything with a text (see, for instance, Bajohr 2024). Yes: we stumble along with the fundamental problem that if we turn out to be wrong about assigning this first-order category, our lovely Marxist readings of what turns out to be a genAI text are—what? Not "true" anymore? (Do genAI's "frames of reference" include economic exploitation?) Not useful? Again: while in relation to genAI the question may appear to be existential, these kinds of decisions about how we relate to a text are basically the same as what we do when we find that an oft-cited memoir is really made up; that an ostensibly Latinx writer's Border novel is possibly written by a writer with a much more ambiguous ethnic heritage; that a Chinese-American poet's poem is really written by a White man. We already have categories whose importance to the discipline is independent of the text: none of us, I think, would be surprised to find an Indigenous viewpoint plausibly represented by a White writer, or, much more basically, a man's perspective by a female author. Reliance on extra- or paratextual markers thus is an overt possibility, and it's as likely to fail with genAI as it has done in the past with ethnic, gender, or class identity. But in any case, nothing much changes.

There is another simple solution: we decide not to differentiate between genAI literature and human literature. Set aside the question why anybody would want to, or indeed, under market conditions, if anybody could continue to write under a regime of genAI literary production: we could just continue to read everything as though it were a human product. That would mean treating all texts equally as texts, no matter their origins, displacing human agency in the making of art in favor of what appears to me to be more theoretically coherent conception of literature. We would treat genAI text like any other intentional output, ascribing (as in the argument

[2] One recent example of a scandal of this kind was the withdrawal from publication in the U.S. of Mia Ballard's horror novel *Shy Girl*, which had already been published in the U.K. earlier by Hachette (now pulped), and before that had been self-published by the author. As Alexandra Alter (2026) reports in the *New York Times*, from the perspective of at least one publisher, genAI usage is "like with plagiarism—you're that the mercy of the author," despite this novel's genAI usage being discovered through AI detection software.

Steven Knapp and Walter Benn Michaels keep making) intentionality to a text because without such an assumption, we really couldn't treat it as text. In that case, nothing about the basic practice of literary studies changes either, although we will have, somewhat inadvertently, signally widened our understanding of what kinds of things can be intentional agents. But that's no matter. As Michaels and Knapp point out, in their response to the post-genAI forum on *Against Theory*, "making judgments about agency is precisely what the practice of interpretation is" (2023). This would also track with the way we professionally treat all texts equally as authored texts, as texts that are primarily the result of a single author's mental processes, despite our knowledge of the social embeddedness of writing. We can, as I've noted above, already hold in abeyance our knowledge of Garcia Marquez's networked creativity to assume that the text speaks with a single voice, one often enough attributed simply to Marquez himself. In either case, nothing much would change for literary studies practice at all. We would continue to produce our interpretations, do our archival work, perhaps try to find out something more about how precisely genAI constructs text.

What, then, are the ways in which we could respond to genAI literary criticism, to genAI interpretations—to the performance not of our object, but of our subject? In part, the avenues open track onto the discussion I've just offered. One option we do have is that we can simply ignore AI's outputs as *performances of literary studies*. We can ignore them, in fact, to any degree of fidelity to actual, human, literary studies output, simply on account of their lack of intentionality—the same kind of choice we have for literature, in other words. Of course, again, we can only do so if we know that they are genAI outputs in the first place. And even then, in a sense, this would be a philosophically more complicated issue, in so far as while we don't have any good inclusionary principles for the category of literature that would force us to attend to a certain text, we really haven't got a good exclusionary principle for literary studies. Or, in simple terms: it may seem tentatively valid, given where our interests with literature lie (the expression of human experience, the registration of social and economic life, the interiority of the psyche, and so on) to consider excluding an agent from this discussion for whom we posit access to none of these issues. But it may seem less correct to exclude that same agent from a field where, in the simplest terms, we emphasize exteriority anyway. What I've above described as a fully text-based evaluation of argumentative plausibility that explicitly excludes attention to who makes the argument seems to give us little principled leeway to exclude genAI from the cohort of our peers.

What follows, then, is the other option, which may need to be the default option for moments, at the very least, where we have no knowledge of an actual author: to accept that genAI literary studies texts are, in fact, viable literary studies, apt performances of the discipline.[3] To do so would, however, fundamentally reshape our sense of our discipline: a more overt acknowledgment that our relationship to our object of knowledge is a bit weird, and the kinds of things that we do have a weird status as outputs. For if genAI could produce Marxist criticism of *Moby Dick*, I think, two things are correct: either it can produce an infinite number of distinct plausible Marxist criticisms of *Moby Dick*, or it can produce a finite number of plausible Marxist criticisms of *Moby Dick*.[4]

If it did the former, we might well question the value of each individual reading as a reading. I do not think we necessarily have to: it is, as we all know, perfectly permissible for disparate and even conflicting interpretations to stand besides each other without thereby impinging on each other's validity. The notion of the infinite, perhaps merely but potentially not, pushes this fundamental axiom of (some) hermeneutics, however. If there are genuinely infinitely many readings, how would we distinguish between their explanatory potential? In fact: does any single one even lay claim to explanatory potential in the first place—is any one of them "knowledge"? Is any of them useful in the world? I would tend to think they're not: infinitely many meanings of *Moby Dick* simply mean that anything, basically, goes, and conversely, nothing really matters.

[3] I am giving admittedly short shrift to the immediate practical problem that we are faced with even now (see Konstantinou 2025), a likely inundation with genAI slop literary studies "papers." The term "slop" describes, in Shaib et al.'s definition, "generic, low-quality content that appears to have been generated by AI" (2025, 1), where quality is a domain-dependent register that can signify relevance, factuality, structure, and even tone (7). In general usage, "slop" also tends to mean something that is readily identified as being AI-generated. In Konstantinou's example, these are, in addition, obviously implausible and faulty attempts at literary studies; in the terms I have tried to employ throughout, they are also if not immediately then with a small amount of effort distinguishable from human writing. This form of existing genAI "literary studies" writing is therefore not, to my mind, of principled interest here—they are not fundamental to the discipline in the way the issues I have raised, I think, are.

[4] I would tend to think that there cannot in fact be an infinite number of plausible interpretations of a necessarily finite text.

One the other hand, if it's the latter, and we have a finite number of plausible readings of *Moby Dick*, then the problem is different: we might have to cope with the problem that all plausible readings of all theoretical persuasions of all texts can just be done by genAI. Rather than adding its voice to the chorus of interpreters, then, genAI would by dint of the rapidity of its production simply eclipse human interpretations. On the one hand, that means we'll have solved literary studies in very much the same way Sam Altman pretends to think genAI can solve physics; on the other, it means that we'll have to rethink what the purpose of our work is—for it will no longer be literary criticism. It may, potentially, still involve the kinds of things which genAI can't easily do: say, visit archives or, especially, teach. But it will not be, I think, output-oriented textual work of any kind. And, more pressingly, this question, unlike the question of our relationship to genAI literature, is perhaps less an intradisciplinary problem but a metadisciplinary one, one less for the discipline to solve as of the discipline itself. In this problem, it's less clear that it will be us who are calling the shots long term. We, for whatever sound epistemological or political or unsound metaphysical reasons may well just ignore genAI's literary output, at least where we can identify it. But the question in the case of our own work is how long we get to do this ignoring before someone on the outside of the discipline begins to ask us about *our* outputs, before someone goes: hang on, what actually is it you're doing? The key point here may be that while the theoretical, philosophical, and epistemological issues genAI literary studies produces are interesting, they pale before the material and concrete questions that emerge from them. We're unlikely to be allowed to retreat into the position where we simply declare non-intentionally produced literary studies texts inadmissible: rather, these texts would confront us inevitably with our own replacement.

I say "genAI produces" here, incidentally, because the point to reply here cannot simply be that any such criticism would still require a human-made prompt. Even in the situation where to get your iterative Marxist reading of *Moby Dick*, you'd have to prompt it to do that reading, your human agency and certainly your scholarship are meaningless. This would also hold true if you had to revise your prompt, or if you had to stitch together a number of answers to different prompts. You'd be replacing academic creative work with curatorial work—editorial work at best. This might still be valuable, but it would also entail a radical reconfiguration of our understanding of what humans are for in literary studies.[5]

The mere possibility of genAI producing our outputs, whether of the most exalted or the most pedestrian kinds, already devalues our outputs now. Already, it asks us to consider what we are doing, and why: already, it asks us to specify what it is that any new Marxist reading of *Moby Dick* actually does, and, indeed, what not just any, but what the best possible reading of *Moby Dick* does. This is a question both for the discipline itself and also the uses of the discipline in the world. How do our outputs matter, *concretely*? How do they matter as human outputs? Who do they matter for? GenAI asks us these questions with as much force as the pocket calculator asked after the value of human computers, and as genAI itself asks after all other textual workers, from law clerks to advertising copy writers to poets. My wager here is the following: the specter of genAI as an acceptable producer of literary studies knowledge return us to the process, to the method, to the doing of literary studies, rather than the outputs it results in. This is one lesson, incidentally, we may take from AlphaGo and AlphaZero. Recall that Lee Sedol, the defeated Go master, retired from Go because he knew he would never be better at Go than the computer. This is valuing an output—winning—over a process—playing. And we might not be inclined to follow down Sedol's footsteps here. Go, of course, still thrives—and so does chess. Both do so because people still value the process of playing either game, including watching others play, as expressions of human capability and as joyous and useful mental processes.

There are echoes here of a number of more recent positions in literary studies discourse. Notably, perhaps, Joseph North's argument that the "future of criticism" (2017, 194; "criticism" taking on a very specific

[5] There is, of course, a basic issue even with only partial uses of genAI—such as the one I've reported from colleagues in a footnote above. You are liable to be caught in what Laurent Dubreuil calls "cognitive path dependence (2025, 77), i.e., by exposing yourself to a suggestion from genAI, you find yourself cognitively limited in what avenues you are willing and able to actively pursue in your further thinking. In one, admittedly science-based example of how this is clearly intransparent even to smart users: in January 2026, the Cologne-based biologist Marcel Bucher complained to Nature Online's career column that, when he lost access to ChatGPT in August 2025, he also lost the "intellectual scaffolding" of two years of "work." While it takes Bucher two years to discover that "these tools were not developed with academic standards of reliability and accountability in mind," he still misses the fundamental point that Dubreuil's framing raises: that, in fact, you are outsourcing the boundaries of thought to genAI even in these cases of using it only for framing "your" work.

meaning in North) will need to go beyond making analyses and to "mobilize those analyses…in a project of systematic cultural intervention," including the need to create a "range of disciplinary sites and resources" (211) beyond what we have right now. North is not, it bears admitting, saying anything here about the uselessness of our outputs; but clearly the rote, everyday academic article, produced from a sense of formal obligation already does not do the kind of work he envisages. What North is hinting at is a reorganization of the discipline that, if it does not abandon its outputs, at least understands them as concretely for something; a sense which, I would agree, it is difficult to sustain in the present, and which it will be harder to sustain in the future. What the challenge of genAI asks us to consider practically is that our outputs simply do not matter: the next reading of *Moby Dick* published in *Early American Literature* and the next interpretation of David Mitchell in *Contemporary Literature* are, as outputs, essentially valueless. What might matter is the process of their making: the act of interpretation, rather than the having of an interpretation. That's not quite as dystopian as the framing Nir Evron gives this horizon: "If LLMs will soon be able to produce creative, historically sensitive, and politically conscious reinterpretations of the past in the service of an imagined future […] we all have more ominous scenarios to contemplate than the extinction of the humanities," he suggests (2024, 318). There is, I think, an important gap between Evron's implied doomsday scenario (which if nothing else also still misses that "creative," "sensitive," and "politically conscious" will remain mere effects of textuality) and the moment we come to realize genAI does creative interpretation—of the kind we, as literary scholars, see ourselves committed to. It's also no more utopian an outcome, I'm sorry to say, than what I failed Katherine Elkins for earlier. Such a devaluation of output is, of course, a significant challenge: output, after all, is what most of the processes by which we are measured as professionals utilize as a proxy for our very quality, our value, as scholars, even beyond publish or perish. Whether it is the number of publications on our CV for practices of hiring or promotion; the usefulness of our books for other peoples' projects and thinking; or simply the way we tend to be introduced at conferences ("she is the author of…"): output rules supreme. No-one cares how we got there; indeed, as the examples of Kramnick and Martus and Spoerhase above show, sometimes we go so far as to proclaim the process of making literary studies almost ineffable, a matter of unconsciously embodied, transcendent flow. But, bereft of outputs as a viable distinction between us and genAI, we would need to rethink this element of doing, rather than of having done, as crucial to the discipline: as the thing to advocate for institutionally, the thing to teach, the thing to hang our hopes on for the future. I do not think we, as a discipline, have a vision of our discipline outside of publication, have a sense of what the discipline could be absent outputs. Neither, admittedly, do I—everything I see around me is too bound up in the market logics of the neoliberal university and the way in which, even absent neoliberalism, scholarly work is tied to productivity. Crucially, here, the easiness with which I can evoke the "we" masks the fact that it's unlikely to be "us" that react to these changes in viability of literary studies project as it stands: it's administrators, politicians, and in the last instance the public that we then need to convince of our utility again.[6] Aarthi Vadde suggests that, apropos of genAI's capacities, "university-based literature, writing, and foreign language instructors can still shape whether and how these technologies are used in the classroom" (2024, 555). It's not entirely clear if Vadde is using simple present for fixed futures here, or means to speak solely about her present moment. Take her to mean the present: perhaps. But already, genAI is, if not forced on them, then less than gently offered to instructors, to professors, as it is to students. It is also questionable whether or not it makes sense to make individual choice the determining instance of genAI's uses. What does my refusal to use genAI do for the discipline? And if Vadde means to speak to the future—to assert that we will always be able to make those choices—that would seem a bit naïve. Without a justification, without a sense of why we should be allowed to resist, of what the point of resistance would be, we will not be able to shape anything much about genAI uses, until we have said something about what our uses are.

To me, it should be clear by now, the point remains: the obverse of all this discussion of what our value is would be to say that if the interpretative work of literary studies is no longer worthwhile in the face of genAI, it never was worthwhile in the first place, certainly not in terms of what kinds of outputs it produces. But, and here's the major interesting wager, perhaps: some of this logic might already pertain now, even without genAI

[6] This is not, to be sure, to suggest that we should adapt ourselves to standards of utility that we do not share. Beyond saving individual careers, nobody much is helped by literary studies successfully arguing that literary studies-trained students are better at neoliberalism, that we aid in people's career prospects, and so on. Rather, I suggest that we should clarify our utility on our own terms, to us, and aim to communicate this sense of societal usefulness to others.

finishing literary studies for us. What is the value of our outputs now, compared to our processes? What work does an interpretation do, aside from being fruitful for further interpretations, for which the same question would pertain anyway? This is what I was driving at in suggesting the moment of genAI is productive of thought: against its foil, we may be able to revalue practices that have become second nature, but may ultimately not be doing any useful work. I say "may" because, of course, I'm not really positing their uselessness here: there may in fact be something useful in the next, and the next, and the next reading of *Moby Dick*, read by the small cadre of readers of a professional academic journal. But we should probably at least entertain the notion that there is not; and that we need to rethink the purpose and practices of the literary studies disciplines fundamentally. If genAI does nothing but make us do that, it will still not be fully worth the sheer expense of energy, the horrible abuses of its capacity to fake and feign, or the still-uncontrolled power it brings to companies largely outside of democratic control. But at least it'll have done *something* useful.

As a prolific producer of outputs, and one who enjoys outputting, that is by no means a conclusion I come to lightly, but it comes with an upside. We can still rejigger the discipline. We can foreground, in lieu of what kinds of outputs we produce, the one thing that appears to be understood, at least within the discipline, as genuinely valuable: our ways of reading. But instead of foregrounding these ways, which elsewhere I have felt confident in calling our "method" (Lanzendörfer 2023, 2025), through what they end up producing, we should foreground them as teachable practices. In this connection, it does indeed become important to come, again, in practice, to an agreement of what kinds of ways of reading texts might be permissible (see Da 2025), of course. What makes literary studies valuable even in an age in which genAI might produce both literary criticism and the literature it produces is the way it reads.

This is precisely what John Guillory sets out when he suggests that close reading is, at heart, little more than a way to open our reasoning to the inspection and contestation by other readers.[7] This process of

[7] Even this little is already a bit more than others offer, though. Da suggests, somewhat idiosyncratically, that close reading is well defined (if potentially only for the occasion of her essay) as "the processing of critical information in real time" (104–105), which seems to be an activity we basically need to take for granted anyway—what Jürgen Habermas has called a "prepredicatively mastered competency" (2023, 116, my own translation)?

contestation can be framed, as Phillip Wegner does in a truly utopian vision for literary studies, as a moment where readers necessarily "occupy the same plane [...] refusing appeals to authority and referring only to the text itself," producing a situation in which "the possibility might ensue of the 'minimal communism' of real and productive dialogue—truly listening to one another rather than [...] just waiting for [our] turn to speak" (2020, 47). At the heart of what I would suggest is a possible future for literary studies thus lies the communal, the directly interpersonal, the active and proximate engagement of other readers with the methods of literary studies that we hold to be valuable. If they are valuable, as methods of reading, to us, then so are they to others: and to communicate them, to validate them, to make them part of more peoples' reading lives, can be a useful future for the discipline.

In saying that, I accept that for Guillory, close reading is necessarily also writing, and that for Wegner, this commons of close-reading contestation of meaning occurs in physical presence—and these two versions are not wholly commensurable, nor very easily translated into practices. Yet I would wager that the moment of genAI is precisely the moment where the idea of a return to the teaching of method, to the exemplification of method, to an education in method might be the most straightforward avenue for relevance that the discipline of literary studies has—and, more importantly, it is an avenue that it has, and should pursue, no matter what the final abilities of genAI will be. This reconceptualization of the practice of literary studies would have us realize that rather than the contestable reading itself, the process of generating such a reading, the careful attention to textual evidence and (potentially) the making of the best possible written version of the argument are the things we might aim for disciplinarily, rather than the publication of yet another reading, yet another monograph. For the imaginary and impersonal audiences of our writings merely imagined as contributions to an ongoing discussion, we would substitute our teaching to real audiences, and actual contributions to the making of "real and productive dialogue."

I end on this hopeful note because, if nothing else, I want to believe that that there is a use to literary studies. GenAI confronts us with the possibility that that use may not, or at any rate no longer, or at *any* rate potentially no longer, lie in producing textual outputs. I'd wager that in our heart of hearts, we've known that for a while. So set aside for now my most maximalist claims for the potentials of genAI, perhaps more designed to get you annoyed and awake than to be fully argued through (perhaps not, though). The moment of genAI cannot but ask of us to rethink that question: where're we at? What changes in our thinking about literature and literary studies given the capacities, both current and extrapolated, if not imagined, of generative AI? If nothing else, I'd wager that if your answer is "nothing," then you've not given it enough thought. And neither, for that matter, have I.

References

Alter, Alexandra. 2026. AI is Writing Fiction. Publishers are Unprepared. *New York Times*, March 19, 2026. Online.

Bajohr, Hannes. 2024. On Artificial and Post-artificial Texts: Machine Learning and the Reader's Expectations of Literary and Non-literary writing. In *The AI Revolution: Speculations on Authorship, Pedagogy, and the Future of the Profession*, edited by Nir Evron and Roi Tortakovsky. Special Issue of *Poetics Today* 45 (2): 331–361.

Bucher, Marcel. 2026. When Two Years of Academic Work Vanished with a Single Click. *Nature.com*. Online.

Collu, Matteo Gioele, et al. 2025. Publish or Perish: Prompt Injection Attacks on LLM-Assisted Peer Review. *arXiv.org*. Online.

Da, Nan Z. 2025. Literary Criticism in the Age of AI. *New Left Review* 155: 103–127, September/October 2025.

Dubreuil, Laurent. 2025. *Humanities in the Time of AI*. Minneapolis: University of Minnesota Press.

Elkins, Katherine. 2024. A(I) University in Ruins: What Remains in a World with Large Language Models? *PMLA* 139 (3): 559–565.

Evron, Nir. 2024. LLMs and the Amazing Shrinking University. In *The AI Revolution: Speculations on Authorship, Pedagogy, and the Future of the Profession*, edited by Nir Evron and Roi Totakovsky, 317–324. Special Issue of *Poetics Today* 45 (2).

Habermas, Jürgen. 2023. Warum nicht lesen? In *Warum Lesen?* edited by Katharina Raabe and Frank Wagner, 99–123. Berlin: Suhrkamp.

Hayles, N. Katherine. 2022. Inside the Mind of an AI: Materiality and the Crisis of Representation. *New Literary History* 53 (4)/54 (1): 635–666.

Knapp, Steven, and Walter Benn Michaels. 2023. Here is a Wave Poem that I Wrote…I Hope You Like It! In *Again Theory: A Forum on Language, Meaning, and Intent in a Time of Stochastic Parrots*, edited by Matthew Kirschenbaum. *Critical Inquiry*, Online.

Knöchelmann, Marcel. 2024. Formal Authorship in the Wake of Uncertain Futures: The Narrative of Publish or Perish in the Humanities. *Research Evaluation* 33:1–13.

Konstantinou, Lee. 2025. Peer Review Paranoia. *The Chronicle of Higher Education*, September 2. Online.

Lanzendörfer, Tim. 2023. The Work of Literary Studies: Interpretation, Argument, and Socioaesthetic Experience. In *Futures of Literary Studies*, edited by Mathias Nilges and Tim Lanzendörfer. Special issue of *Textual Practice* 37 (2): 221–239.

Lanzendörfer, Tim. 2025. Education in Method: A Minimalist Manifesto for Public Literary Studies. *Public Humanities* 1:1–11.

Marx, Karl, and Friedrich Engels. 1973. *Grundrisse*. London: Penguin.

Marx, Karl, and Friedrich Engels. 1990. *Capital. Volume I*, 1990. London: Penguin.

Marx, Karl, and Friedrich Engels. 2010. The German Ideology. In *Marx-Engels Collected Works*, Vol 5: April 1845–April 1847. London: Lawrence & Wishart, 19–452.

North, Joseph. 2017. *Literary Criticism: A Concise Political History*. Cambridge: Harvard University Press.

Pasquinelli, Matteo. 2023. *The Eye of the Master. A Social History of Artificial Intelligence*. London: Verso.

Shaib, Chantal, Tuhin Chakrabarty, Diego Garcia-Olano, and Byron C. Wallace. 2025. Measuring AI 'Slop' in Text. *ArXiv.org*. Online.

Vadde, Aarthi. 2024. Inside and Outside the Language Machines. *PMLA* 139 (3): 553–558.

Wegner, Phillip. 2020. *Invoking Hope: Theory and Utopia in Dark Times*. Minneapolis: University of Minnesota Press.

Bibliography

Alberto, Isabelle Rose, et al. 2025. The Rise of 'Vibe Science': How AI Threatens Scientific Rigor. *TechRxiv.org*. Online.

Alter, Alexandra. 2026. AI is Writing Fiction. Publishers are Unprepared. *New York Times*, March 19, 2026. Online.

Altieri, Charles. 2024. Modes of Intelligence. In *The AI Revolution: Speculations on Authorship, Pedagogy, and the Future of the Profession*, edited by Nir Evron and Roi Tortakovsky. Special Issue of *Poetics Today* 45 (2): 207–214.

Anker, Elizabeth, and Rita Felski, eds. 2019. *Critique and Postcritique*. Durham: Duke University Press.

Anthropic. 2025. Equipping Agents for the Real World with Agent Skills. Online.

Bajohr, Hannes. 2023a. Niemand schreibt allein (Nachwort zu *(Berlin, Miami)*). In *Berlin, Miami*, 239–267. Berlin: Matthes & Seitz.

Bajohr, Hannes. 2023b. *Schreibenlassen. Texte zur Literatur im Digitalen*. Berlin: August Verlag.

Bajohr, Hannes. 2023c. When in Doubt, Go to the Beach. In *Again Theory: A Forum on Language, Meaning, and Intent in a Time of Stochastic Parrots* (blog), edited by Matthew Kirschenbaum, June 27. Online.

Bajohr, Hannes. 2024. On Artificial and Post-artificial Texts: Machine Learning and the Reader's Expectations of Literary and Non-literary writing. In *The AI Revolution: Speculations on Authorship, Pedagogy, and the Future of the Profession*, edited by Nir Evron and Roi Tortakovsky. Special Issue of *Poetics Today* 45 (2): 331–361.

T. Lanzendörfer, *AI and the Challenge to Literary Studies*,
https://doi.org/10.1007/978-3-032-25526-6

Barthes, Roland. 1977/1967. The Death of the Author. In *Image-Music-Text*, 142–148. New York: Fontana.

Baßler, Moritz. 2021. Der neue Midcult: Vom Wandel populärer Leserschaften als Herausforderung der Kritik. *Pop. Kultur und Kritik* 18:132–149.

Bates, David W. 2024. *A History of Natural Intelligence: Thinking with Machines from Descartes to the Digital Age*. Chicago: University of Chicago Press.

Bender, Emily M., Timnit Gebru, Angelina McMillan-Major, and Shmargaret Shmitchell. 2021. On the Dangers of Stochastic Parrots: Can Language Models Be Too Big?. In *FAccT '21: Proceedings of the 2021 ACM Conference on Fairness, Accountability, and Transparency* (March), 610–623.

Berry, David M. 2023. The Explainability Turn. *DHQ* 17 (2).

Bertram, Lillian-Yvonne, and Nick Montfort. 2024. *Output: An Anthology of Computer-Generated Text, 1953–2023*. Cambridge and London: MIT Press and Denver and New York: Counterpath.

Binder, Jeffrey M. 2022. *Language and the Rise of the Algorithm*. Chicago: University of Chicago Press.

Bosse, Heinrich. 2014. *Autorschaft ist Werkherrschaft: Über die Entstehung des Urheberrechts aus dem Geist der Goethezeit*. Paderborn: Fink.

Bourdieu, Pierre. 1996. *The Rules of Art: Genesis and Structure of the Literary Field*. Cambridge: Polity Press.

Breithaupt, Fritz. 2023. *The Narrative Brain: The Stories Our Neurons Tell*. New Haven: Yale University Press.

Brouillette, Sarah. 2024. The Author as Social Production. (Review). *Studies in the Novel* 56 (1): 99–1045.

Bucher, Marcel. 2026. When Two Years of Academic Work Vanished with a Single Click. *Nature.com*. Online.

Burrow, Colin. 2019. *Imitating Authors: From Plato to Futurity*. Oxford: Oxford University Press.

Castelvecchi, Davide. 2025. DeepMind and OpenAI Models Solve Maths Problems at Level of Top Students. *Nature*, July 24. Online.

Catani, Stephanie, ed. 2023. *Handbuch Künstliche Intelligenz und die Künste*. Berlin: DeGruyter.

Cavell, Stanley. 2009. Must We Mean What We Say? In *Must We Mean What We Say?* 1–43. Cambridge: Cambridge University Press.

Chakrabarty, Tuhin, Jane C. Ginsburg, and Paramveer Dhillon. 2025. Readers Prefer Outputs of AI Trained on Copyrighted Books over Expert Human Writers. *Columbia Law Research Paper* 5605670. Online.

Chiang, Ted. 2024. Why A.I. Isn't Going to Make Art. *The New Yorker*, August 31. Online.

Childress, Clayton. 2017. *Under the Cover: The Creation, Production, and Reception of a Novel*. Princeton: Princeton University Press.

Chollet, Francois. 2019. On the Measure of Intelligence. *arXiv.org*. Online.

Clune, Michael. 2019. *A Defense of Judgment*. Chicago: University of Chicago Press.
Collu, Matteo Gioele, et al. 2025. Publish or Perish: Prompt Injection Attacks on LLM-Assisted Peer Review. *arXiv.org*. Online.
Comitta, Tom. 2025. *People's Choice Literature: The Most Wanted & Unwanted Novels*. New York: Columbia University Press.
Crawford, Kate. 2021. *Atlas of AI: Power, Politics, and the Planetary Costs of Artificial Intelligence*. New Haven: Yale University Press.
Da, Nan Z. 2025. Literary Criticism in the Age of AI. *New Left Review* 155: 103–127, September/October 2025.
Davis, Joshua, et al. 2024. The Temperature Feature of ChatGPT: Modifying Creativity for Clinical Research. *JMIR Hum Factors*, March 8.
DeCosmo, Leonardo. 2022. Google Engineer Claims AI Chatbot Is Sentient: Why That Matters. *Scientific American*, July 12. Online.
Dreyfus, Hubert L. 1992. *What Computers Still Can't Do*. Cambridge: MIT Press.
Dreyfus, Hubert L., and Stuart E. Dreyfus. 1988. Making a Mind versus Modelling the Brain: Artificial Intelligence Back at a Branchpoint. *Daedalus* 117 (1): 15–43.
Dubreuil, Laurent. 2025. *Humanities in the Time of AI*. Minneapolis: University of Minnesota Press.
Dugan, Holly, and Dolsy Smith. 2024. Untimely Models. *PMLA* 139 (3): 516–521.
Dziri, Nouha, et al. 2022. On the Origin of Hallucinations in Conversational Models: Is it the Datasets or the Models? In *Proceedings of the 2022 Conference of the North American Chapter of the Association for Computational Linguistics: Human Language Technologies*, 5271–5285.
Eaglestone, Robert. 2019. *Literature: Why It Matters*. London: Polity.
Eagleton, Terry. 2008. *Literary Theory: An Introduction*. Minneapolis: University of Minnesota Press.
Elam, Michelle. 2023. Poetry Will Not Optimize; or, What is Literature to AI. *American Literature* 95 (2): 281–303.
Elkins, Katherine. 2024. A(I) University in Ruins: What Remains in a World with Large Language Models? *PMLA* 139 (3): 559–565.
Evron, Nir. 2024. LLMs and the Amazing Shrinking University. In *The AI Revolution: Speculations on Authorship, Pedagogy, and the Future of the Profession*, edited by Nir Evron and Roi Totakovsky, 317–324. Special Issue of *Poetics Today* 45 (2).
Evron, Nir, and Roi Tortakovsky, eds. 2024. *The AI Revolution: Speculations on Authorship, Pedagogy, and the Future of the Profession*. Special Issue of *Poetics Today* 45 (2).
Feige, Daniel Martin. 2025. *Kritik der Digitalisierung: Technik, Rationalität und Kunst*. Hamburg: Meiner.
Felski, Rita. 2009. *The Uses of Literature*. New York: Wiley.
Felski, Rita. 2015. *The Limits of Critique*. Chicago: University of Chicago Press.

Fletcher, Angus. 2021. Why Computers Will Never Read (or Write) Literature. *Narrative* 29 (1): 1–28.

Fletcher, Angus. 2022. Why Computer AI Will Never Do What We Imagine It Can. *Narrative* 30 (1): 114–137.

Fletcher, Angus. 2024. Shakespeare Didn't Brainstorm: Why Literature Proves That There's More to Intelligence than AI. In *The Routledge Handbook of AI and Literature*, edited by Will Slocombe and Genevieve Lively, 125–135. London: Routledge.

Foucault, Michel. 1998/1969. What is an Author? In *Aesthetics, Method, and Epistemology*, 205–222. New York: The New Press.

Franklin, Samuel. 2023. *The Cult of Creativity: A Surprisingly Recent History*. Chicago: University of Chicago Press.

Gadamer, Hans-Georg. 2004. *Truth and Method*. London: Routledge.

Gil, Alex. 2023. On the Uses of Text beyond Intention. In *Again Theory: A Forum on Language, Meaning, and Intent in a Time of Stochastic Parrots* (blog), edited by Matthew Kirschenbaum, June 28. Online.

Gould, Stephen Jay. 1996. *The Mismeasure of Man*. New York: Norton.

Grankowski, Alex, Stephen M. Downes, and Partick Forber. 2024. LLMS are Not Just Next Token Predictors. *arXiv.org*. Online.

Guillory, John. 2022. *Professing Criticism: Essays on the Organization of Literary Study*. Chicago: University of Chicago Press.

Guillory, John. 2025. *On Close Reading*. Chicago and London: University of Chicago Press.

Habermas, Jürgen. 2023. Warum nicht lesen? In *Warum Lesen?* edited by Katharina Raabe and Frank Wagner, 99–123. Berlin: Suhrkamp.

Harris, Mark. 2012. TV's Best Talker: Aaron Sorkin on The Newsroom, Sorkinism, and Sounding Smart. *Vulture*. Online.

Hayles, N. Katherine. 2022. Inside the Mind of an AI: Materiality and the Crisis of Representation. *New Literary History* 53 (4)/54 (1): 635–666.

Hayles, N. Katherine. 2024. Don't Ban AI From Your Writing Classroom; Require It! *Poetics Today* 45 (2): 259–265.

Hayot, Eric. 2014. Academic Writing, I Love You. I Really Do. *Critical Inquiry* 41 (1): 53–77.

Heaven, Will Douglas. 2023. Google DeepMind Used a Large Language Model to Solve an Unsolved Math Problem. *MIT Technology Review*. Online.

Henricksen, Leah. 2024. Conversations with No One. In *The AI Revolution: Speculations on Authorship, Pedagogy, and the Future of the Profession*, edited by Nir Evron and Roi Tortakovsky. Special Issue of *Poetics Today* 45 (2): 291–299.

Jin, Weina, Xiaoxiao Li, and Ghassan Hamarneh. 2023. Why is Plausibility Surprisingly Problematic as an XAI Criterion? *arXiv.org*. Online.

Juhl, Peter. 1981. *Interpretation: An Essay in the Philosophy of Literary Criticism*. Princeton: Princeton University Press.

Kalai, Adam Tauman, Ofir Nachum, Santosh S. Vempala, and Edwin Zhang. 2025. Why Language Models Hallucinate. *arXiv:org*. Online.

Kirschenbaum, Matthew. 2023. Again Theory: A Forum on Language, Meaning, and Intent in the Time of Stochastic Parrots. In *Again Theory: A Forum on Language, Meaning, and Intent in a Time of Stochastic Parrots*, edited by Matthew Kirschenbaum. *Critical Inquiry*, Online.

Kirschenbaum, Matthew, and Rita Raley. 2024. AI and the University as a Service. *PMLA* XXX:1–12.

Klimczak, Peter, and Christer Petersen, eds. 2023. *AI—Limits and Prospects of Artificial Intelligence*. Bielefeld: transcript.

Knapp, Steven, and Walter Benn Michaels. 1982. Against Theory. *Critical Inquiry* 8 (4): 723–742.

Knapp, Steven, and Walter Benn Michaels. 2023. Here is a Wave Poem that I Wrote…I Hope You Like It! In *Again Theory: A Forum on Language, Meaning, and Intent in a Time of Stochastic Parrots*, edited by Matthew Kirschenbaum. *Critical Inquiry*, Online.

Knöchelmann, Marcel. 2024. Formal Authorship in the Wake of Uncertain Futures: The Narrative of Publish or Perish in the Humanities. *Research Evaluation* 33:1–13.

Konstantinou, Lee. 2025. Peer Review Paranoia. *The Chronicle of Higher Education*, September 2. Online.

Kramnick, Johnathan. 2023. *Criticism and Truth*. Chicago: University of Chicago Press.

Kraus, Kari. 2023. A View from the Periscope. In *Again Theory: A Forum on Language, Meaning, and Intent in a Time of Stochastic Parrots*, edited by Matthew Kirschenbaum. *Critical Inquiry*, Online.

Kwa, Thomas, et al. 2025. Measuring AI Ability to Complete Long Tasks. *arXiv.org*. Online.

Labatut, Benjamin. 2023. *The Maniac*. London: Penguin.

Lanzendörfer, Tim. 2023. The Work of Literary Studies: Interpretation, Argument, and Socioaesthetic Experience. In *Futures of Literary Studies*, edited by Mathias Nilges and Tim Lanzendörfer. Special Issue of *Textual Practice* 37 (2): 221–239.

Lanzendörfer, Tim. 2024. Participatory Literary Studies and the Question of Public Method. In *Participation in American Culture and Society*, edited by Philipp Löffler, Margit Peterfy, Natalie Rauscher, and Wolf Werner, 223–242. Heidelberg: Winter.

Lanzendörfer, Tim. 2025a. You Can't Say That: The Serious Limits of Literary Studies Creativity. *Creativecritical.net*. Online.

Lanzendörfer, Tim. 2025b. Education in Method: A Minimalist Manifesto for Public Literary Studies. *Public Humanities* 1:1–11.

Lanzendörfer, Tim. forthcoming-a. The Labor of Literary Studies.

Lanzendörfer, Tim. forthcoming-b. What Does Literary Studies Know?

Lanzendörfer, Tim. forthcoming-c. Facetious Criticism; Or: Why We Don't Have to Mean What We Say.

Lanzendörfer, Tim, and Mathias Nilges. 2025. Preface: Futures of Literary Studies, Revisited. In *Futures of Literary Studies*, edited by Mathias Nilges and Tim Lanzendörfer, x–xiii. Cham: Palgrave Macmillan.

Lanzendörfer, Tim, and Corinna Norrick-Rühl, eds. 2020. *The Novel as Network: Form, Idea, Commodity*. Cham: Palgrave Macmillan.

Lewinsky, Charles. 2024. *Täuschend Echt*. Zürich: Diogenes.

Leypoldt, Günter. 2016. Degrees of Public Relevance: Walter Scott and Toni Morrison. *Modern Language Quarterly* 77 (2): 369–393.

Leypoldt, Günter. 2025. *Literature's Social Lives: A Socio-Institutional History of Literary Value*. Oxford: Oxford University Press.

Lindsey, Jack, et al. 2025. On the Biology of a Large Language Model. *Transformer Circuits*. Online.

Lorentzen, Christian. 2024. Literature Without Literature. *Granta* 168. Online.

Lu, Chris, et al. 2024. The AI Scientist: Towards Fully Automated Open-Ended Scientific Discovery. *arXiv*, September 1.

Macherey, Pierre. 1978. *A Theory of Literary Production*. London: Routledge.

Marcinkowski, Michael. 2024. There Has Never Been an Intelligent Literature. In *The Routledge Handbook of AI and Literature*, edited by Will Slocombe and Genevieve Lively, 113–124. London: Routledge.

Marraccini, A. V. 2023. *We the Parasites*. London: Boiler House Press.

Martus, Steffen, and Carlos Spoerhase. 2022. *Geistesarbeit. Eine Praxeologie der Geisteswissenschaften*. Frankfurt: Suhrkamp.

Marx, Karl, and Friedrich Engels. 1973. *Grundrisse*. London: Penguin.

Marx, Karl, and Friedrich Engels. 1990. *Capital. Volume I*. London: Penguin.

Marx, Karl, and Friedrich Engels. 2010. The German Ideology. In *Marx-Engels Collected Works*, Vol. 5: April 1845–April 1847, 19–452. London: Lawrence & Wishart.

McGurl, Mark. 2009. *The Program Era: Postwar Fiction and the Rise of Creative Writing*. Cambridge: Harvard University Press.

Meier-Vieracker, Simon. 2024. Uncreative Academic Writing: Sprachtheoretische Überlegungen zu Künstlicher Intelligenz in der akademischen Textproduktion. In *KI:Text. Diskurse über KI-Textgeneratoren*, edited by Gerhard Schreiber and Lukas Ohly, 133–144. Berlin: DeGruyter.

Monot, Pierre-Héli. 2023. Robopathen und Robopathinnen aller Länder…wenn die KI die Drehbücher schreibt. *Merkur* 903:84–92.

Moretti, Franco. 1998. *Atlas of the European Novel 1800–1900*. London: Verso.

Moss, Adam. 2024. *The Work of Art: How Something Comes from Nothing*. New York: Penguin.

Navas, Eduardo. 2022. *The Rise of Metacreativity: AI Aesthetics After Remix*. London: Routledge.

Nersessian, Anahid. 2022. For Love of Beauty? Literary Criticism in Troubled Times. *New Left Review* 133 (134): 179–196.

North, Joseph. 2017. *Literary Criticism: A Concise Political History.* Cambridge: Harvard University Press.

Ottman, Klaus. 1986. Jeff Koons 1986 Interview. Quoted from https://libbys-niche.blogspot.com/2009/08/jeff-koons-1986-interview.html; originally in *Journal of Contemporary Art*, October 1986.

Pasquinelli, Matteo. 2023. *The Eye of the Master. A Social History of Artificial Intelligence.* London: Verso.

Perlow, Seth. 2024. Generative Theories, Pretrained Responses: Large AI Models and the Humanities. *PMLA* 139 (3): 548–522.

Porter, Brian, and Edouard Machery. 2024. AI-Generated Poetry is Indistinguishable from Human-Written Poetry and Is Rated More Favorably. *Nature: Scientific Reports* 14. Online.

Poston, Ted. 2024. Experience, Plausibility, and Evidence. *Philarchive.org.*

Putnam, Hilary. 1981. *Reason, Truth, and History.* Cambridge: Cambridge University Press.

Reisner, Alex. 2025. Search LibGen, the Pirated-Books database That Meta Used to Train AI. *The Atlantic.* Online.

Rettberg, Scott. 2019. *Electronic Literature.* Cambridge: Wiley.

Roach, Rebecca. 2025. *Programming Literature.* Oxford: Oxford University Press.

Roach, Rebecca, Pierre-Héli Monot, and Tim Lanzendörfer. forthcoming. The Plausibility of Academic Forms in the Age of their Computational Reproducibility. Under review.

Ruby, Ryan. 2024. *Context Collapse: A Poem Containing a History of Poetry.* New York: Seven Stories Press.

Santana-Acuña, Alváro. 2020. *Ascent to Glory: How One Hundred Years of Solitude Was Written and Became a Global Classic.* New York: Columbia University Press.

Sawyer, Keith N., and Danah Henriksen. 2024. *Explaining Creativity: The Science of Human Innovation.* Oxford: Oxford University Press.

Schmidt, Paul G., and Amnon J. Meir. 2023. Using Generative AI for Literature Searches and Scholarly Writing: Is the Integrity of Scientific Discourse in Jeopardy? *arXiv.org.* Online.

Schüttpelz, Erhard. 2023. *Deutland.* Berlin: Matthes & Seitz.

Sinkyin, Dan, and Johanna Winant, eds. 2025. *Close Reading for the 21st Century.* Princeton: Princeton University Press.

Sinykin, Dan. 2023. *Big Fiction: How Conglomeration Changed the Publishing Industry and American Literature.* New York: Columbia University Press.

Siraganian, Lisa. 2023. On Accidental and Parasitic Language. In *Again Theory: A Forum on Language, Meaning, and Intent in a Time of Stochastic Parrots*, edited by Matthew Kirschenbaum. *Critical Inquiry*, Online.

Slocombe, Will, and Genevieve Lively, eds. 2024. *The Routledge Handbook of AI and Literature*. London: Routledge.

Thorne, Sarah. 2019. Hey Siri, Tell Me a Story: Digital Storytelling and AI Authorship. *Convergence: The International Journal of Research into New Media Technologies* 26 (4): 808–823.

Turing, Alan M. 1950. Computing Machinery and Intelligence. *Mind* 59 (236): 433–460.

Vadde, Aarthi. 2024. Inside and Outside the Language Machines. *PMLA* 139 (3): 553–558.

Van Woudenberg, René. 2019. *The Epistemology of Reading and Interpretation*. Cambridge: Cambridge University Press.

Wakabashi, Daisuke, and Jin yu Young. 2024. Defeated by AI, a Legend in the Board Game Go Warns: Get Ready for What's Next. *New York Times*, July 10. Online.

Wegner, Phillip. 2020. *Invoking Hope: Theory and Utopia in Dark Times*. Minneapolis: University of Minnesota Press.

Williams, Raymond. 1977. *Marxism and Literature*. Oxford: Oxford University Press.

Winko, Simone, et al. 2024. *Praktiken des Plausibilisierens. Untersuchungen zum Argumentieren in literaturwissenschaftlichen Interpretationstexten*. Göttingen: Universitätsverlag Göttingen.

Winterson, Jeanette. 2025. OpenAI's Metafictional Short Story About Grief is Beautiful and Moving. *The Guardian*, March 12.

Wooldridge, Michael. 2020. *A Brief History of Artificial Intelligence: What it Is, Where We Are, and Where We Are Going*. New York: Flatiron Books.

Zeraoulia, Rafik. 2025. Why Mathematicians Resist AI: Between Rigor, Risk, and Opportunity. *ArXiv.org*. Online.

Zhou, Eric, and Dokyun Lee. 2024. Generative AI, Human Creativity, and Art. *PNAS Nexus* 3:1–8.

Žižek, Slavoj. 2008. *The Sublime Object of Ideology*. London: Verso.

Zylinka, Joanna. 2023. Art in the Age of Artificial Intelligence. *Science* 381 (6654): 139–140.

Index[1]

[1] Note: Page numbers followed by 'n' refer to notes.

T. Lanzendörfer, *AI and the Challenge to Literary Studies*,
https://doi.org/10.1007/978-3-032-25526-6

GPSR Compliance

The European Union's (EU) General Product Safety Regulation (GPSR) is a set of rules that requires consumer products to be safe and our obligations to ensure this.

If you have any concerns about our products, you can contact us on ProductSafety@springernature.com

In case Publisher is established outside the EU, the EU authorized representative is:

Springer Nature Customer Service Center GmbH
Europaplatz 3
69115 Heidelberg, Germany

Batch number: 10837145

Printed by Printforce, the Netherlands